THE ACCLAIMED* NOVEL ABOUT TEENAGE ALCOHOLISM AND DRUNK DRIVING

Binge

now points the way to a better life

D1297448

ngeII:
Recovery

with the most promising alcoholic recovery program ever developed:

EIGHT STEPS TO SOBRIETY AND A BETTER YOU

(page B 1)

*Chosen as a best book for young adults by The American Library Association, The New York Public Library, and The National Council of Teachers of English.

Binge II:

Recovery

EIGHT STEPS TO SOBRIETY AND A BETTER YOU

Brandy Baker

Charles Ferry (b. 10-8-27), a *Who's Who* author, was born in Chicago, raised in Wisconsin, and now lives in Rochester Hills, Michigan, with his wife, Ruth, and their beloved Belgian sheepdog, Emily Anne. To learn more about him, consult: *Something about the Author Autobiography Series*, vol. 20; *Children's Literature Review*, vol. 34; *Something about the Author*, vol. 92, all by Gale Research, Inc.; and *International Authors and Writers Who's Who*, 16th edition, International Biographical Center, Cambridge, England.

ALSO BY CHARLES FERRY

A Fresh Start	Proctor, 1996
Binge	Daisy Hill 1992
One More Time!	Houghton, 1985
Raspberry One	Houghton, 1983
O Zebron Falls!	Houghton, 1977
Up in Sister Bay	Houghton, 1975

Binge II:
Recovery

EIGHT STEPS TO SOBRIETY AND A BETTER YOU

Charles Ferry

DAISY HILL PRESS
Rochester, Michigan

Publisher's Cataloging-in-Publication
(Prepared by Quality Books, Inc.)

Ferry, Charles, 1927 -
  BingeII : recovery / EIGHT STEPS TO SOBRIETY AND A
  BETTER YOU / Charles Ferry. — 2nd ed.
  p. cm.
  SUMMARY: Eighteen-year-old Weldon comes to in a
  hospital and must confront the aftermath of a
  tragic drinking and driving binge in this novel,
  with a nonfiction appendix outlining eight steps
  for recovering from alcoholism.
  LCCN: 99-94635
  ISBN: 0-9632799-8-X
  1. Drunk driving—Juvenile fiction. 2.
Alcoholism—Juvenile fiction. 3. Self-help
techniques—Juvenile literature. I. Title

  PZ7.F42Bin 1999   [Fic]
                      QB199-330

Copyright © 1999 by Charles Ferry

DAISY HILL PRESS
PUBLISHED IN THE UNITED STATES OF AMERICA

To Berl Olswanger's loving daughter
Anna Girl
with deep thanks

INTRODUCTION

I'm going to let Joseph Lucas introduce this book. Who is Joseph Lucas? Our lives touched when he sent me the following letter:

10-26-98

Dear Sir:

Hello! My name is Joseph Lucas. I am 24 years old. I am an alcoholic currently serving an 18-month to 5-year prison sentence for theft related to drugs and alcohol.

I recently read an article in my hometown newspaper (Erie, Pennsylvania, *Daily Times*) about your battle in life, plus about your writing.

The article has inspired me very much. I give you much credit on your new ways. Reading the article has taught me that if a man like you can rise above the horrors of his life, so can I.

I am writing to ask for a copy of Binge. I think it would be very educational to read. When I'm done, I will see to it that it gets passed around and put into the prison library.

Thank you very much.
Joseph Lucas, DP5003
P.O. Box 200
Camp Hill, PA 17001-0200

In addition to *Binge*, I sent Joseph a copy of my 1996 title, *A Fresh Start*, in which I first introduced my *Eight Steps*. (That book is available from Proctor Publications, P.O. Box 2498, Ann Arbor, MI 48106, 1-800-343-3034, paperback, $8.95).

This is an excerpt from Joseph's next letter:

... After reading *Binge*, I lay in my cell that night and cried. I let it all out and felt very good.

I have started to work *The Eight Steps*. I plan on starting an *Eight Steps* group when I get paroled.

Drugs and alcohol have messed up my life in the past. I hurt my family, lost my girlfriend of five years, who has my son, lost trust from many people, plus my credit went down the tubes.

Today, I look at all that as the past. Today is the beginning not the end, which your *Eight Steps* made me realize.

Thank you...

I have scores of letters like that, from people of all ages, from all walks of life.

Maybe I'll receive one from you.

Charles Ferry

CONTENTS

BingeⅡ:

Recovery

EIGHT STEPS TO SOBRIETY
AND A BETTER YOU

He was having that dream again, the Loon Lake dream. It was the summer that he and Livvie Buhl turned twelve. They were in the hayloft at Buhl Farm, and Livvie let him slip his hand inside of her panties. His heart throbbed with excitement, feeling the softness, the dampness.

"Just think, Weldon," Livvie whispered into his ear, "maybe next summer we'll have our own secret place."

But something was wrong with this dream. When he glanced toward the back of the loft, he saw a policewoman, sitting on a bale of hay. No, it wasn't a bale of hay; it was a chair, in a hallway, seen through a doorway. A man in a robe rolled by in a wheelchair, and a woman in a white uniform was coming through the doorway. A nurse?

He was awake now. He felt sore all over, and his feet hurt terribly, especially the right one. He could hear funny sounds, a soft hissing and a steady *bleep, bleep, bleep*. Where was he? What was he doing here? His head seemed to be bandaged, and there was something under his nose, like a thin mustache, only it extended around his cheeks. He tried to raise his arms to feel it, but they seemed to be tied down. The nurse noticed his movements and came to the bed. She was a small, dark-haired woman, with large blue eyes and a pleasant smile.

"So you're finally awake?" she said, adjusting the plastic tube that was taped to his left arm.

"Yes," he said.

It came out ye*th*. He ran his tongue over his gums and discovered that his front teeth were missing, both uppers and lowers. His mouth tasted foul, and his face was swollen. His whole body felt swollen, as though he were in someone else's skin and it didn't fit.

"Where am I?" he asked. His voice sounded raspy, and it hurt him to breathe.

"A hospital," she said. "Bridgton Memorial." She removed the spongy loops that had been restraining his arms.

"You don't need these now, Weldon. We didn't want you to pull out the IV in your sleep."

She had called him Weldon. They knew his real name. What else did they know? Had they found the other wallet? It was ruined, his reunion with Livvie, his plan for a new life at Loon Lake, all of it. And he had come so close. He started to scratch his chest and felt several little cups attached to wires.

"What're these?"

"That's the bleeping you hear." The nurse lifted his hospital gown and removed the suction cups. "We've been monitoring your heart."

As she worked, she explained the rest of his situation. The IV that hung from a stand next to the bed would be continued indefinitely; it was supplying him with nourishment and antibiotics. The tent-like arrangement at the foot of the bed was there to keep pressure off of his feet, both of which had been injured.

"How bad?"

"Pretty bad."

"What about this?" He tapped the bandage that covered his head.

"Contusions and lacerations," she said. "Not too serious, but they had to shave your head to treat them."

The plastic tubes in his nostrils, the source of the hissing sound, were providing him oxygen, she said.

"Your ribs were badly bruised. Not broken, but you haven't been breathing as deeply as you should, and it's important to oxygenate your blood as much as possible."

If he had to urinate, he should go right ahead, she said; a catheter had been inserted into his urethra, draining into a bag that hung from the bedframe. For bowel movements, she would bring a bedpan.

"How long have I been here?" Weldon shuddered slightly; his right foot was throbbing horribly.

"Since Thursday night. Today's Saturday. It's almost one."

"Did I see a policewoman out in the hall?"

She adjusted the IV tube again, avoiding his eyes. "I'm afraid you did," she said. "You're a--a police prisoner."

A prisoner? It started to come back to him. Coming over that last hill, he had hit something. There was a series of thuds, like quilted pins being struck by a bowling ball. Then the T-bird had gone into a skid. He remembered a huge tree coming out of the blackness, then nothing.

"Here, let's see if we can make you more comfortable," the nurse said, raising the head of the bed. "By the way, I'm Miss Wetherby, your day nurse."

"Nice to meet you, Miss Wetherby." Weldon attempted a smile, then remembered the missing teeth and closed his mouth.

"We'll be seeing a lot of each other," she said.

"How long will I be here?"

"It depends on you." She began to attach some metal things to the bed. "I'd say two weeks or so. Move your arm just a bit, please. That's it."

As she worked, Weldon tried to assess his situation. Maybe it wasn't too bad. A stolen car--he'd probably get probation, even if they knew about the credit cards. His record was clean. Oh, he'd been busted a couple of times for bad checks, but both times his mother had made them good, and the charges had been dropped. Maybe there was still hope. When it was over, he would get a job somewhere and pull himself together. After he'd saved some money, he would get his teeth fixed, buy a cheap used car, and finally make it to Loon Lake. It would take a while, but that was all right; it would take time for his hair to grow back. Maybe this rotten experience would turn out to be a plus. He would tell Livvie the whole story. She would be touched by the risks he'd taken to be with her again and realize that after all these years, the flame still burned

3

brightly in his heart.

But two weeks in this dumb hospital was going to be hard to take. He wondered if Miss Wetherby would sneak him a pint of Jack Daniel's? He had read about a hospital in Chicago where they let special patients have champagne with their dinner. He had plenty of money, and whiskey was medicinal, wasn't it? A painkiller. He needed it. He deserved it.

"--We're going to have to work like a team, Weldon," Miss Wetherby was saying. "I can take care of your body from the outside, but you've got to tell me about the inside. All right?"

"Okay," Weldon said.

"Fine. First, do you feel nauseated?"

"My stomach feels funny, but it's not like I'm going to throw up or anything."

"Good. What about your eyes? Is your vision blurred or are you seeing double?"

"No."

"Very good. Now I know you're in pain. How bad is it?"

"Terrible. My feet. Especially the right one."

Miss Wetherby gave him an uneasy look.

"Was the right one hurt the worst?"

"Wel-l, in a way."

"In what way? Did it take more stitches than the left one?"

"Quite a few more."

"Well, stitches aren't too bad. When will they come out? When will I be able to walk to the bathroom? I don't want any bedpans."

"That's hard to say, Weldon."

"What's hard about it? The bones aren't broken, are they?"

Miss Wetherby drew a deep breath and bit her lip.

"I hate to be the one to tell you, Weldon, but you--you no longer have a right foot."

Weldon's mouth fell open. He stared at Miss Wetherby in disbelief.

4

"No right foot?" He said it in a whisper first, then loudly, angrily. "No right foot? What the fuck do you mean, no right foot?" The words came out in a slobber; blood from his torn gums splattered his gown. "I can *feel* my right foot! I can wiggle my toes!"

Miss Wetherby went to the foot of the bed. "That's known as the phantom limb sensation," she said. "It will feel like that for a few days."

She pulled the blanket back from the foot cradle. Weldon's right leg, heavily bandaged and resting on a pillow, was about six inches shorter than his left one, which was also bandaged.

"Oh, Christ." He said it in a groan, half-crying.

"Doctor Weng said he had no choice," Miss Wetherby said. "It was shredded. It was all he could do to save the left one. The medics said the transmission came through the flooring."

Weldon stared at the leg as though it wasn't his. There must've been a mistake. The foot was probably in cold storage somewhere; when it was fixed, they would sew it back on. He'd read about operations like that. No, they did that with livers and kidneys, not feet. Oh, God, it was really gone. Mama, Mama, they cut off my foot! But there was no Mama to turn to. He had burned that bridge behind him; he had burned all of his bridges. What was he going to do? How could he get through life without two feet? Mama, Mama, MAMA---

"I'm terribly sorry, Weldon. I truly am. You seem like a nice enough young man, but you've gotten yourself into a horrible situation. And a lot of other people, I might add."

Miss Wetherby went to the call box that was in the wall to the left of the bed and pressed the button.

"Bernice? Martha in four-oh-four. Tell Doctor Weng he's awake, but give me a few minutes to get him cleaned up. Is Ella Mae there?---"

Weldon had detected a note of censure in her voice. A lot of other people--what had she meant by that? His parents?

There was nothing horrible about their situation. His mother managed a gift shop in Springhurst, and his father had just been promoted to chief district engineer of his company, a big pipeline firm. That's why they'd gone to Maui, to celebrate. Rick Wessell, the man whose car he'd stolen? His situation certainly wasn't horrible. Sure, he had been inconvenienced, but he still had two good feet and a big new job.

"Ella Mae, will you please cover for me with my other patients? I may be here for quite a while. Keep your eye on that boy in four-eleven, and--"

Four-eleven. That had been his room number at the Briarwood. What a comedown. From the Barclay Room and sparkling Burgundy to *this*--and in just two days.

While Miss Wetherby talked, he glanced around the room, trying to grasp the hopelessness of his circumstances. He had never been in a hospital room before, not even to visit. It was a cheerless room, the walls a drab green, the floor a worn gray. To his left was a row of windows that cranked open. The windows gave a view of a wooded hill that was ablaze with the reds and golds of autumn. Bridgton was a lovely town. They had passed through it many times on the way to and from Beechers Grove and the cottage at Loon Lake. On one trip, they had eaten at a Howard Johnson's on the edge of town. His sisters, Laurie and Denise, had ordered pistachio ice cream; he had had rainbow ripple. Afterward, they had all played video games in the children's lounge. It seemed so long ago. And now, he was in Bridgton again, lying in a hospital bed, under police guard and with no right foot. He felt a numbness inside. How was he going to get out of this mess? *How?* He wished he had a drink; with a few drinks, he'd think of something. But *what?*

Wait. Maybe, just maybe, there was still a chance. His Grandfather Yeager had fought in World War II, in the Battle of the Bulge, and had lost a leg. He had come home on crutches, a hero. Maybe he would be a hero in Livvie's eyes, a wounded warrior who had fallen in the struggle to regain his lost love. He remembered a scene from an old war movie on the late show, a crippled fighter pilot and his lover, clinking glasses by candlelight. Maybe, just maybe--

"Here, Weldon, you'll feel better when you've freshened up a bit." Miss Wetherby had brought soap, towels, and a basin of warm water to the bed. "You'll have to rinse your mouth with peroxide and water. We don't want to risk using a brush on your torn gums."

She had attached an overhead support to the guard rails of the bed; it had a hand grip that resembled a little trapeze.

"Grab this and pull yourself up," she said. "I've got a clean gown for you. But be careful of your IV and oxygen tubes."

"Can you give me something for my pain?" Weldon asked her. "It's pretty bad."

"Doctor Weng will have to prescribe it. He'll be here shortly. You'll like him, but don't let his casual manner fool you. He's one of the best orthopaedic surgeons in the state."

Dr. Weng, a small man with a stethoscope dangling from around his neck, breezed into the room as Miss Wetherby was patting Weldon's cheeks dry.

"Sorry I'm late," he said, with a smile and a wave for each of them. "Heavy traffic in Emergency."

A stalk of celery protruded from a pocket of his blue lab coat. He took a bite of celery and went to the foot of the bed; his chewing made a loud crunching sound.

"I've had to eat on the run," he explained, taking the patient's chart from Miss Wetherby, "and you know how I like celery, Martha."

She laughed. "And raw carrots," she said, "and raw cabbage. You're a regular rabbit. 'Weng the Wabbit,' they call you in Cardiology."

"Weewee?" Dr. Weng replied, doing an imitation of Elmer

Fudd. As he scanned the chart, he lifted the blanket from the foot cradle and inspected Weldon's bandages. "Let's see, now, vital signs good, no infection . . ."

"He knows about the foot," Miss Wetherby said, removing the basin and towels from the bed.

Dr. Weng sighed. "It's just as well," he said. "It spares me the grief. I'm sure he's in considerable pain." He wrote something on the chart. "Fifty MGs of Demerol should do it."

Miss Wetherby went to the nurses' station and returned with a medicine cart. She unlocked the narcotics drawer and prepared the injection.

"Grab the trapeze and roll over a bit, Weldon," she said. "This goes in your right hip. There. Better?"

"Oh, yes," he said, breathing a sigh of relief.

"Repeat it every four hours, Martha," Dr. Weng said taking another bite of celery. "More often, if the pain is severe."

"Yes, doctor."

Dr. Weng leaned over the bed and extended a hand to Weldon.

"With a name like 'Weldon,'" he said, smiling, "what does a guy use for a nickname?"

Weldon didn't know what to make of this celery-eating physician. "He doesn't," he said. "They call me 'Junior' at home."

"That's simple enough," Dr. Weng said. "Well, Junior, all things considered, you're doing fairly well. Oh, you'll hurt for a while, but it's like hitting yourself on the head with a hammer: It feels good when you stop. Squeeze my hand, please, as hard as you can. Good. Now try it with the left one. Ouch, not so hard. Very good. Now I'm going to ask you some silly questions. Just bear with me. What's your full name?"

"Weldon Edmund Yeager, Junior." Weldon hated his name. He should've been a Tom or a Jack or a Bill, but, no, he had to have *his* name.

"And where are you from?"

"Springhurst, Illinois."

"What state are you in now?"

"Michigan."

"Who discovered America?"

"Columbus."

"Close enough. It was really the Vikings. Now hold out your right arm and touch your nose with the tip of your index finger. Like this. Good. Now with your left arm. Good."

He took an ophthalmoscope from his breast pocket and shone it in Weldon's eyes.

"Look straight ahead, Junior. That's it. It's nice to see you with your eyes open. I thought you were going to sleep for a week. How long had you been drinking, anyway?"

Weldon shrugged. "I just had a few beers," he said.

"Really? Must've been strong beer. Now look to the left. Your blood alcohol content was point-two-four. At point-one-oh you're legally intoxicated."

"Do the police know that?"

"Of course. The police know everything. Lieutenant Becker will be here soon to talk with you. Now look to the right. We wanted him to wait for a day or two, but he insisted. All right, Junior, grab the trapeze and sit up as straight as you can."

Dr. Weng examined Weldon's entire body, listening, tapping, pressing, and talking as he did so.

"You're a very lucky young man, Junior."

"I don't feel lucky."

"No, I suppose you don't, but you're alive."

"That's lucky?"

"Most people would think so."

"With only one foot and a cop guarding the door?"

"Listen, Junior, I know you're in a hell of mess, but you think you've got troubles? My uncle was in China during the Cultural Revolution. I could tell you stories that would curl

9

your hair."

"But I'm not in China."

"No, you're in Bridgton, Michigan. And I could tell you Bridgton stories that would curl your hair. Martha could I see his flow chart for a minute? Thanks. Last year, on prom night, four local kids got wiped out in a car wreck. Cold sober. Does it hurt when I press there? Good. But you were spared. With your point-two-four BAC, you were spared. Makes you think, doesn't it. Okay, Junior, you can lie back now."

He stuffed the stethoscope into a pocket.

"The point I'm making is this: You can lie there and wallow in self-pity, or you can start making the most of your good fortune. I minored in philosophy in college, and I've never forgotten the immortal words of Aristotle. He said that a man with a hole in his pocket invariably feels cocky."

Miss Wetherby struggled to keep her composure, and even Weldon, despite his grim situation, smiled.

"No, Aristotle didn't say that," Dr. Weng said. "He said, 'This, too, shall pass away.' Or something like that. And it will, Junior. So start counting your blessings and--"

There was a commotion out in the hall and the sound of angry voices.

"What the hell is that?" Dr. Weng said, going to the door.

It was a television news crew, arguing with the police-woman--a man with a camera mounted on his shoulders and a young woman in a red blazer, holding a microphone. As Dr. Weng opened the door, they spotted Weldon.

"There he is!" the woman said. The camera started whirring, and the two of them tried to move into the room.

"Out!" Dr. Weng ordered them, blocking the way. "This is a hospital, not a studio."

"But we drove all the way from Grand Rapids to get this footage," the woman said.

"And you'll drive all the way back without it," Dr. Weng

said. "Officer, no more intrusions, hear?"

"Sorry, doctor. These two must've sneaked up on the surgery elevator."

Dr. Weng closed the door and grimaced. "Damn TV crews," he said. "They think they own the world."

Weldon had watched the scene in amazement. A TV crew for *him?* For a stolen car and the business with the credit cards? It didn't make sense.

"What was that all about?" he asked Dr. Weng.

"Unfortunately, Junior, you're the biggest story in town."

"But *why?*"

"That's police business, not hospital business. You're Lieutenant Becker's prisoner, our patient. We're supposed to keep our personal feelings to ourselves, and sometimes it isn't easy, especially in a case like yours. Just be thankful that I'm not Lieutenant Becker."

Weldon was jarred by the doctor's strong remarks. Again, a tone of censure. Had his true feelings just shown through? Were he and Miss Wetherby being nice to him just because that was their job?

Dr. Weng smiled and patted Weldon's shoulder. "Sorry, Junior," he said. "I sort of got carried away, but TV crews bother me."

"Sure," Weldon said. "I understand." But his anxiety was mounting. Obviously, he was in bad trouble, really bad. Not just the stolen car and the credit cards, but something else, something much worse. But *what?*

Dr. Weng consulted Weldon's chart again.

"Martha, do we have plenty of potassium in his IV?"

"Yes, doctor. Two thousand MGs."

"Junior would probably like us to add a pint of vodka, but he'll do better with good nutrition." He looked at his watch. "Well, I guess that's it. Lieutenant Becker will be here soon. He'll miss the big game, and his son's playing tailback this

11

year."

"Really?" Miss Wetherby said, moving to the row of windows. "Which one is that -- Billy?"

"Marvin. Billy Becker's the one at Notre Dame."

Miss Wetherby cranked open one of the windows. "It's a bit stuffy in here," she said. "These older rooms just don't have good ventilation."

A smell of burning leaves came in the window, and there were sounds of band music and a crowd cheering.

"Football," she explained to Weldon. "The stadium's just beyond that ridge."

"A college game?" he asked her.

"Bridgton High. It's their homecoming."

"Today's homecoming at Springhurst, too."

"Really?" she said. "Did you ever play football, Weldon? You look the type."

"For a while."

Dr. Weng looked in at him with new interest. "Hey, I figured you were some kind of athlete," he said. "You've got the build. What position?"

"Place-kicker. You know, field goals, extra points."

"Right-footed?"

Weldon nodded.

Dr. Weng shook his head sadly. "Well, Junior, your field goal days are over, but you'll be able to dance, jog, skate. They've done wonders in prosthetics."

"How many years did you play, Weldon?" Miss Wetherby asked him.

"Three. In my senior year, I sort of, you know, got interested in other things." He didn't tell her that he'd been kicked off the team. His grades were falling, and he and his buddy Art Rothery had been caught with "strawberry pop" in the locker room. The pop was really red wine in a Pepsi bottle.

"Martha?" --it was the call box--*"Lieutenant Becker is*

here."

Miss Wetherby turned to Dr. Weng. "Are we ready for him?"

"As ready as we'll ever be."

"Send him in, Bernice."

Dr. Weng patted Weldon's shoulder again and winked. "Keep a liff upper stiff, Junior."

"A what?"

"A stiff upper lip. Just remember the immortal words of Plato. 'When in doubt, plead the fifth amendment.'"

Lieutenant Becker was a tall black man, wearing a blue tweed jacket and gray flannel trousers. His short hair and thick mustache were both flecked with gray. He was accompanied by an officer in a tan gabardine uniform, who set a large black carrying case on one of the chairs.

"Good afternoon, nurse, doctor," the lieutenant said, nodding to them. "Yeager," he said to Weldon, "I know you're hurting, but this has to be done."

"But *why* does it have to be done?" Dr. Weng said. "The boy's just had an amputation."

"I know, I know," Lieutenant Becker said. "But the prosecutor wants some answers. The whole town wants some answers."

"May I help you, lieutenant?" Miss Wetherby asked.

"We've got to book him, print him, and get some temporary mug shots. Officer Bibich will need something firm for taking his prints, and I'll need an electric outlet for my tape recorder. Is that telephone connected?"

"Yes, sir."

"Make sure it is disconnected after I leave. On second thought, I'll see to it myself."

The room began to resemble a police station. Miss Wetherby brought a bed table, on which Officer Bibich placed a large ink pad and an arrest form. Then he set up a tripod at the foot of the bed and mounted a camera and a strobe light on it. "Sit up as straight as you can," he ordered Weldon, draping a numbered slate around his neck— *BCSD89750*. "All right, fella, look straight at the camera. Good. Now turn your head all the way to the left. That's it. Now to the right." As the strobe light flashed, a sinking sensation went through Weldon's stomach. This can't be happening, he thought. It's all a bad dream. I'll wake up in a Best Western, have a few Jack Daniel's and ginger ale, and everything will be all right.

The policewoman came in from the hall to help with the fingerprinting. "Hold that form down tight, Mary. I don't want to smudge it. Relax your fingers, fella. I said relax them, damn it! That's better. Here, clean your fingers with this." He produced a bottle of solvent and a soft cloth. Miss Wetherby brought soap and water from the bathroom.

"Here, Weldon, let me help you."

As she washed his hands, a vision flashed through Weldon's mind, of his mother rubbing salve on his hands after he had burned them at a barbecue at Loon Lake. That was the summer he and Livvie swam across Up Holly Bay, the widest bay in the lake. They had done it at dawn, when there was a mist on the bay and the water was smooth as glass. His mother had followed them in a rowboat. On the way back, they had sung funny songs, their voices drifting out over the water.

> Row, row, row your boat,
> Gently down the stream.
> Merrily, merrily, merrily, merrily,
> Life is but a dream.

"I'm finished, lieutenant," Officer Bibich said. "What about you? Think you'll be long?"

"An hour or two, Nick. Why don't you relieve Mary for a bit? She hasn't eaten yet. And check on those kids in Intensive

Care."

"Yes, sir."

"And, Nick? See if you can find out if the game has started."

"Right."

Lieutenant Becker turned to the others. "All right, I've got work to do," he said. "Everyone out--except the prisoner, of course."

"And the prisoner's nurse," Miss Wetherby said.

The lieutenant gave her an impatient look. "You don't seem to understand, Miss Wetherby. This is police business."

"I understand perfectly, lieutenant. But this is our hospital, not your squad room. I'm not leaving my patient alone in a traumatic situation."

Lieutenant Becker turned to Dr. Weng. "Doctor, will you please explain--"

"Sorry, lieutenant," Dr. Weng said. "This room is her domain. If she says she's staying, she's staying." He and Officer Bibich started out the door. "I'll tell Bernice, Martha."

"Thank you, doctor."

Weldon was glad that Miss Wetherby was staying; Lieutenant Becker wasn't.

"I'm not used to having spectators at an interrogation," he said to her, frowning. "I trust you'll make yourself conspicuous by your silence."

Miss Wetherby moved a chair around to the right of the bed, next to the TV set, which was mounted on a metal arm that swung out from the wall. "I'll be no problem at all, lieutenant," she said. "Weldon, let me know if you need anything."

"Yes, ma'am."

Lieutenant Becker's tape recorder was on the bedside stand, to the left of the bed. He unbuttoned his jacket and sat down. Weldon could see the butt of his gun, which he carried in a shoulder holster.

15

"All right, Yeager," he began. "You have the right to remain silent. Anything you say can and will be used against you in a court of law. Understand?"

Weldon felt numb. "Ye*th, th*ir."

"And you have the right to talk to a lawyer and to have a lawyer present. If you can't afford a lawyer, the court will appoint one. Do you understand that?"

"Yes, sir." Weldon sensed that this was a man to treat with respect. Politeness and courtesy had gotten him out of a few jams in the past, but he didn't know about Lieutenant Becker.

"Now, in this state, Yeager," the lieutenant went on, "you're an adult at the age of eighteen. Except for the Illinois police and the FBI, we haven't notified anyone that you're in custody. We aren't required to. You're entitled to one phone call. Do you want to call your parents?"

"They're away on a trip."

"Whereabouts?"

"Hawaii." He wouldn't call them even if they were at home. He wouldn't give them the pleasure of gloating. The bridges were burned. It was their decision; they had locked him out.

"Any brothers or sisters?"

"Two sisters. They're away at college." Laurie was a senior at Minnesota; Denise was in her second year at Southern Illinois. They would be glad he was out of their hair. Denise had always envied him his collection of old Simon & Garfunkel albums, and Laurie had never forgiven him for catching her making out with some guy on the family room couch. Afterward, he had sent in her name to receive a pamphlet on abortion. Her mother had seen it when it arrived. "But mother, I'm *not* pregnant!" Laurie had screamed, in tears.

"Is there anyone else you want to call?"

"No, sir."

"Suit yourself," Lieutenant Becker said. Weldon noticed

that there was a thin scar on his chin. "Okay, I've read you your rights. Do you want to make a statement?"

"Yes, sir." Be cooperative, Weldon thought. That was his only hope of getting a break.

"Freely and without duress?"

"Yes, sir." If he was courteous and cooperative, he would be a cinch to get probation.

"Without a lawyer present?"

"Yes, sir." What good would a lawyer do him? They had him red-handed. Besides, getting a lawyer would just delay things, and Becker was anxious to get to that damn football game. No, he would kill him with kindness. That way, he would soon be out of this mess and ring-a-ding-doo again.

"All right, let's get down to business." Lieutenant Becker reached to the carrying case for something. "Yeager, do you know why you've been under police guard?"

"Not exactly."

"Maybe you'd like to read your publicity?"

He handed Weldon a copy of a newspaper, the *Bridgton Chronicle*.

DRUNK DRIVER MOWS DOWN FOUR STUDENTS
Two Dead, Two Critical

Two Hillgrove College students were killed outright and two others critically injured Thursday night when they were struck by a stolen car driven by an Illinois man who was trying to elude police.

The dead were identified as William Koehler, 20, of Traverse City, and Marilyn Copple, 18, of Cadillac.

Lt. Howard Becker of the Bridgton County Sheriff's Department said the accident happened at 10:34 on Campus Drive. The students, who held part-time jobs at the Hillgrove Student Union, were returning to their dorms, he said.

"It was a black, misty night," Becker said. "Witnesses said

the car came over a hill doing about 80 and hit the kids before they even saw it. Then it spun out of control and hit a tree."

Becker identified the driver as 18-year-old Weldon E. Yeager, Jr., of Springhurst, Illinois, who is listed as being in serious but stable condition at Bridgton Memorial Hospital, where he is a police prisoner.

The injured victims, who are in Intensive Care at Bridgton Memorial, were identified as Richard D. Svoboda, 19, of Battle Creek, and Olivia Anne Buhl, 18 of Loon Lake.

Weldon stared dumbly at the article. So the quilted pins had been people. He had killed two of them and run down Livvie Buhl, the love of his life. Oh, Jesus God Almighty.

"The paper doesn't say anything about the kids you killed," Lieutenant Becker said. "Bill Koehler was going to Oxford next semester, as an exchange student. I understand he was quite a scholar--"

> *But what was she doing at Hillgrove? When they were kids, they had talked of going to State or the U. of M. Then he remembered. Her mother had gone to Hillgrove. He should've remembered that; he should've remembered a lot of things.*

"The Copple girl's mother has been working two jobs to keep her daughter in college. Now she can take it easy--"

> *While he had been despairing over an amputated foot, Livvie had been in this very hospital, fighting for her life. How had this all happened? How? If only he had a drink. He couldn't think straight without a drink.*

"And it doesn't list the charges that have been filed against you. Car theft, DWI, reckless driving--"

The paper had run a picture of Livvie. It appeared
to be a yearbook photo. She looked much as he had
expected she would, the face a little fuller, the hair
a little darker, but the same gleaming eyes and wide
smile. He hoped she hadn't been disfigured; he
hoped she wasn't suffering too much.

"--larceny, and second-degree murder. Two counts--so far."

He was filled with remorse. If he had two good feet, he would leap out the window. A four-story fall ought to kill him. No, he had to see Livvie first and tell her he was sorry. after that, he didn't care what happened.

"Before we begin, Yeager, I want a few personal details. Your place of birth?"

"Beechers Grove, Michigan."

"Your driver's license is two years old. How tall are you now?"

"Five-eleven."

"Eyes, blue. Hair, blonde. Any distinguishing scars, before those you got in this accident?"

"A scar on my right hand."

"That's all?"

"Yes, sir." Weldon's slurred speech embarrassed him. Y*eth, th*ir. Y*eth, th*ir.

"Yeager, I want you to understand that a transcript of your statement will be sent to Illinois; they've got a hold on you for car theft and a few other items. A copy will also go to Judge Breakey at district court; you'll be arraigned before him as soon as you're able to use a wheelchair. And another will go to the FBI; they may want to do something about interstate credit card fraud. But I doubt it. By the time you get out of Jackson, the FBI and Illinois will have forgotten all about you."

"Jackson?"

"Jackson Prison. The big one. I'd say you'll get twenty years, fifteen if you're lucky."

Weldon had read about Jackson Prison. Some of the older convicts carried knives and sodomized the younger ones. Well, he wouldn't be alive long enough for them to do that to him. After he saw Livvie, he'd get to a window -- somehow.

"An officer will bring over the personal items found in the car to find out which are yours and which are stolen."

"Everything's his," Weldon said.

"Everything?"

"Except some clothes I tossed into the trunk."

"That simplifies things." Lieutenant Becker took a list from his pocket and scanned it. "Let's see -- three suitcases, two garment bags, four cardboard boxes of miscellaneous personal belongings. What about the clothes you were wearing when we brought you in ?"

"His."

Lieutenant Becker paused and gave Weldon a hard look. "You were on top of the world, weren't you?" he said. "Were his neckties to your liking? His shoes?"

Weldon didn't say anything. A drum roll echoed from the stadium, followed by the crashing of a bass drum. The game had probably begun. He hadn't minded being kicked off the football team. It was more fun being a spectator, sitting in the stands and sipping Coke spiked with Jack Daniel's, feeling the warm glow spread through his body. "Hey, Yeager!" the other kids would yell to him. "Save us a snort!" At one game, he had sneaked in--

"Pay attention, Yeager!" The lieutenant was still going over the list. "There was a personal computer in the trunk, a Tandy, and some floppy disks. Maybe the computer can be repaired, but the disks were mangled. You probably wiped out a lot of his work."

"I'm *thorry*."

20

"Sure you are."

"Will Rick be coming out here to get his things?"

"No, which is lucky for you. Now that we've got them identified, we'll ship them to him tonight, air express. His insurance company is handling matters here."

He continued with the list. "Two wallets, three driver's licenses--Mr. Wessell's, your real one, and your fake one. It's a pretty good fake. Who did it?"

"A guy at a print shop back home."

"Not bad, if you don't look closely. Well, let's get down to business."

He clipped a small microphone to Weldon's hospital gown.

"Miss Wetherby, is there anything your patient will require before we begin?"

"Not right now, lieutenant," she replied. "Weldon, don't hesitate to tell me if you need anything. You're overdue for a bowel movement."

"Ye*th*, ma'am."

Lieutenant Becker turned on the tape recorder.

County of Bridgton
SHERIFF'S DEPARTMENT
1210 River Road, Bridgton, Michigan 49223

PRISONER: Yeager, Weldon Edmund, Jr.
CASE NO.: 89750-B
OFFICER: Becker
CHARGES: 148.63/329.20/274.56

BECKER: Let the record show that the prisoner has been informed of his rights and has waived his right to have a lawyer present. Correct, Yeager?

YEAGER: Yes, sir.

BECKER: All right, Yeager, that was quite a binge. Tell me all about it.

YEAGER: What do you want to know?

BECKER: Everything. Start at the beginning. Where did you steal the car?

YEAGER: At a motel near Chicago. I forget the name.

BECKER: Does the Slumber Inn on Dempster Street in Skokie ring a bell?

YEAGER: Yes, sir. I think that was it. You know about it?

BECKER: The Skokie police took care of that end of it. You'd better pray you never run into Mr. Wessell again. He'll kill you. You left him stranded with nothing but his underwear.

YEAGER: I left him some pizza.

BECKER: A regular Good Samaritan. Let the record show that the automobile under discussion is a two-door Thunderbird, model and serial number on file, owned by Richard C. Wessell formerly of Santa Clara, California, and presently of New Britain, Connecticut. Where did you meet him, Yeager?

YEAGER: At a bar near Springhurst. The Purple Parrot. A buddy and me were having a few drinks, and we, you know, got talking to this guy.

BECKER: And that's how it started? A few friendly drinks?

22

YEAGER: Yes, sir.

No, it had started before that. He thought of the series of events that had conspired to put him in the Purple Parrot at ten o'clock that Tuesday night. If Mr. Montague, his English teacher, hadn't been out to get him, he would have graduated with his class and not still be in high school doing makeups. If he hadn't been fired at the Burger King, he would have made good that withdrawal at the automatic teller before his father found out.

If, if, if.

If he had made out with Peggy Stipe that night, he wouldn't have gotten back to the Purple Parrot till later. He'd had Peggy in the back of Art Rothery's van with all her clothes off and been unable to perform. Again.

"Some stud," Peggy had said, hooking her brassiere. "Where're my panties?"

Peggy had made him take her home.

"But Art's waiting for us at the Parrot."

"TV is more fun than you," she had said. "Betty Kurtzman told me about you. All show and no go."

But he wasn't all show. It was just a problem of pacing, of pacing his drinks. Unless he'd been drinking, he couldn't muster up the courage to make advances to a girl. And it was important that the girl be drinking; otherwise it was no good. "Ugh, you smell like a brewery," she would say, and push him away. But if they were both drinking, it was lovely. He was a regular Casanova--clever, witty, charming, ring-a-ding-doo. Drinking gave him an edge, a cool, attractive edge; but if he went beyond that point, he wilted. Because of that, he'd had only one success, and even then, the girl had laughed at him and called him a wimp. The trick was to drink himself just to the edge and then taper off. He hadn't mastered that trick yet, but he was working on it. If his pacing had been better with Peggy Stipe, he wouldn't have gotten back to the Parrot until at least eleven.

If, if, if.

But the most crucial *if* of all had involved Rick Wessell himself. If he had turned off his parking lights, their paths never would have crossed. He had dropped off Peggy and was pulling into the parking lot at the Purple Parrot, when he noticed the taillights shining on a blue Thunderbird with California plates. The driver appeared to be on a trip; a lot of luggage was piled up on the backseat.

"Hey, Herbie!" he called to the bartender as he entered the crowded, smoky Parrot. "Some guy with a T-bird left his lights on."

He elbowed his way up to the bar and ordered a Bud. A Bruce Springsteen number was playing on the jukebox, and several couples were on the small dance floor, rocking.

"Your sidekick's playing shuffleboard," Herbie said as he served Weldon his beer. "And winning a few bucks, too."

"He must be improving," Weldon said, letting the beer foam up in his glass. "I've been coaching him."

He took a deep drink of the beer and tried to forget Peggy Stipe. The Purple Parrot was his favorite spot, a rustic place with a beamed ceiling and walls decorated with art deco posters and blowups of old Humphrey Bogart movie advertisements. Along one wall, there was a table shuffleboard. After he had gotten his fake ID, Weldon had occasionally cut his sixth-period class and spent a few pleasant hours at the Parrot, playing shuffleboard for drinks or cash and always winning.

"You're too damned good at that game," Herbie had once told him. "You oughta spot the other guys some points."

Weldon suspected that Herbie knew that his and Art's IDs were fakes. He himself could easily pass for twenty-one, especially if he wore dress clothes, but Art couldn't. Herbie didn't seem to mind. Business was business, he often said.

He took his drink to an empty table near the shuffleboard

table.

"Weldon, baby!" Art Rothery waved to him. "Didja score?"

Weldon smiled and made a circle with his thumb and forefinger.

"You know me," he said, tossing Art the keys to his van. "The dollies write me thank you notes."

Art, who was short and rotund, grinned from ear to ear. "You macho son of a buck," he said. "Tell me all about it when we get home tonight. Okay?"

"Sure thing, Artie."

"Hey, Yeager!"

It was Herbie, calling to him from the bar and pointing to a man who was coming toward Weldon, a nice-looking man, about twenty-four, Weldon guessed, wearing a gray corduroy jacket, tan chino trousers, and a white button-down shirt with no tie. There was an Ivy League look to him, Weldon thought, even in casual clothes, and he wondered what he was doing in the Purple Parrot. He came straight to the table, smiling, and stuck out a hand.

"I'm Rick Wessell, Weldon," he said. "Hey, I owe you a drink for telling Herbie my parking lights were on."

"Aw, it was nothing, Rick," Weldon said, shrugging.

"What do you mean, nothing? Most people would've ignored it, and I would've had a dead battery. What're you drinking?"

"Jack Daniel's and ginger ale," Weldon said, pushing aside the beer.

"Hey, that's my drink, too." Rick Wessell sat down and signaled a waiter. "Isn't that neat? Already we've got something in common."

And that's how it began. Rick was a hell of a nice guy, pleasant, generous, outgoing, the kind of person that you'd appreciate having as a friend. He loved a party and had a corny but funny sense of humor. *"Do you know what Beethoven's doing in his grave? Decomposing."* Ha, ha. *"Did you put the cat out? Why, was he on fire?"* And he had a clever way of transposing the consonants of words. Santa Clara became *Clanta Sara,* Jack Daniel's, *Dack Janiel's,* and his car was a *Bunderthird.*

He and I hit it off right away. His Ivy League look was genuine; he was a graduate of Yale. Originally from Boston, he had been working in California and was now on his way back East to take a new job in Connecticut. He had made a sidetrip to Springhurst to look up a girl he'd known in college, but she had moved away. He had stopped by the Parrot to use the phone and had decided to stay for a few drinks before finding a motel.

"I should've called her before I left California."

"Whereabouts in California?"

"Santa Clara."

"Hey, Silicon Valley."

"Right."

"What company? Apple? Atari?"

"Helios," he said.

Our drinks had arrived; I was glad to be drinking whiskey instead of beer.

"Helios?" I read *Time* and *Newsweek* regularly and knew a little about a lot of things. As a result, I had learned how to ask knowledgeable questions and get people talking. "Let's see, Helios--they're into artificial intelligence, aren't they?"

"That's my specialty," Rick said. "Are you into high-tech, Weldon?"

"Me?" I laughed. "Hell, no. I'm only eighteen. I've got a fake ID."

"Really?" Rick was surprised. "You sure had me fooled. Are you in college?"

"Not till February," I said. "The University of Iowa. I was late in applying, so they can't take me until then."

"Why Iowa?"

"Well, I had my choice of some good schools. I scored over fourteen hundred on the SAT." (Which was true.) "But Iowa has a great writers program. I'm going to be a novelist."

"Hey, that's wonderful!" Rick said. "I've always wanted to write, but I just don't have the talent. Been published yet?"

"A few short stories and poems," I said. "You know, in smaller magazines." (All of my submissions had been rejected, but one editor had written me an encouraging letter.) "I'm working on a novel now."

Rick signaled for another round of drinks. I reached for my wallet, but he insisted on paying. I felt relieved; my parents had left me only fifty dollars to last for two weeks, and I was already down to seventeen bucks. But my financial prospects were about to brighten.

The Purple Parrot was jumping. The jukebox was blaring, and the dance floor was jammed. Art Rothery came over to our table from the shuffleboard.

"Hey, Weldon, some of the guys over there want to play for money. Doubles."

"You and me?"

"I gotta get home. I've got an eight o'clock class in the morning." Art attended a local community college.

"I'll play with you, Weldon" Rick Wessell offered. "I was once shuffleboard champ of the Bulldog Bar in New Haven."

"But how'll I get home? Art's driving."

"No problem," Rick said. "I'll take you home."

"There you go," Art said. "I'll leave the side door unlocked for you, Weldon. Okay?"

"Okay," I said. "But expect me when you see me."

Rick and I started over to the shuffleboard table.

"Is Art your brother?" he asked me.

"Just a friend. My folks're away on a trip, and I've been staying at Art's house. It simplifies things, you know, meals,

27

laundry."

Rick was a champ, all right. We took on all challengers, at five bucks a head, and won every game. Then someone complained to Herbie that we were hogging the board, and we had to give it up. Rick was really pleased with himself.

"I haven't had this much fun since I was in college," he said as we found seats at the bar and ordered more drinks. "Too bad they don't have a pool table. I'm a regular hustler at pool."

"A bar over on Rand Road has one," I said. "But they close at two, and it's already one-fifteen."

"Do any places stay open later than that?"

"Howard Street," I said. "The joints down there are open till four."

Howard Street was a district of topless bars and x-rated movie houses on the northern fringe of Chicago. I'd never been there, but I was sure some of the places would have pool tables.

Rick looked at me and laughed. "And I was going to hit the sack early," he said. "But what the hell, I might as well make a night out of it. I don't have to report to my new job till Thursday. What about you, Weldon?"

"No problem." I had an afternoon makeup class, but I would cut it. "I can sleep all day if I want."

Rick raised his glass in a toast. "Well, buddy," he said, "here's to Stroward Heet."

"To what?"

"Howard Street."

We laughed ourselves silly. We were on a great party, a classic, and I didn't want it to end.

But the party was to be short-lived. Weldon felt very good, keen, alert, as though he had gotten his second wind and could drink for days. But Rick Wessell, who had been on the road since six that morning, was showing signs of fatigue. They were tooling down Dempster Street in the blue T-bird when

28

Rick's head began to nod and his handling of the car became erratic. Also, his speech was becoming slurred.

"Hate t'poop out on ya, buddy," he said, turning abruptly into a motel, "but I'm startin' t'see double."

Weldon felt his heart sink. The party was ending before it had hardly got started. "But how'm I gonna get home?"

"No problem. I'll get us a dubba--" Rick broke wind. " 'Scuse me. A *double*. You c'n sack out here, and I'll run ya home in the mornin'. Jeez, those drinks hit me all of a sudd'n." He broke wind again. " 'Scuse me."

Weldon couldn't believe what was happening. A marvelous party with an Ivy League man who had accepted him as an equal was ending. Instead of the gaiety and excitement of Howard Street, he would spend the rest of the night in this third-rate motel. And tomorrow? That dumb makeup class, with the other kids making smart remarks behind his back. *"He's the dummy who didn't graduate."* Shit. He wondered if Rick was gay, but there had been no indication of that. To the contrary, he'd talked about how he had made out with the Springhurst girl in New Haven. *"Oh, what a sweet piece she was!"*

The motel room, a dingy, poorly lighted room had twin beds. Rick threw his gray topcoat on the only chair and started to take off his jacket.

"But aren't you gonna bring in one of your bags, Rick?"

"In the mornin'," Rick said, unbuttoning his shirt. "Lissen, Weldon, make sure I get your address, okay? One of m'dad's best friends is a litta . . . a lit-er-ar-y agent. I'm gonna tell him 'bout you."

"Hey, that's great, Rick," Weldon said, grateful that at least one good thing would come of this aborted party.

Rick was sitting on the edge of a bed now, taking off his shoes. Watching him, Weldon wondered why he himself was so sober and a neat guy like Rick Wessell was so drunk.

"You hungry, Weldon?"

"A little."

"Ah'm starved. Only had a Big Mac f'r supper." Rick took his car keys from the nightstand and tossed them to Weldon, who was still standing. "We passed a pizza place 'ways back. Wanna go get us one?"

Weldon began to perk up. A chance to drive the T-bird! And he was sure the pizza place had a bar.

"Large or small, Rick?"

"Large, with extra pepp'roni. And there's a pint o' booze in the glove compartm'nt. Bring it in, and we'll have a l'l nightcap, okay?"

"*Okay!*" Weldon eagerly zipped his windbreaker and went to the door. Maybe the party wasn't over yet. "Be back in a flash, Rick, baby."

"Okay, buddy."

BECKER: Now let me get this straight. Mr. Wessell tossed you his car keys and told you to get him a pizza?

YEAGER: Yes, sir.

BECKER: And you expect me to believe that?

YEAGER: It's the truth.

BECKER: Maybe. A polygraph will decide that. You used no force?

YEAGER: No, sir.

BECKER: You didn't grab his car keys when he wasn't looking?

YEAGER: No, sir.

BECKER: All right, so he tossed you the keys, and you proceeded to steal his car?

YEAGER: No, I didn't do it then. I stole it later.

BECKER: I'm confused. Go back to the time you left the room.

The motel was set back a ways from the road. It was a cold, clear October night, with a bright moon. Weldon shivered slightly as he unlocked the car. Good football weather, he thought. He would have to set aside enough money for a good party after the homecoming game Saturday. Football parties were the best parties of all. He had once kicked the winning field goal in a championship game, and at the party afterward, girls had fallen all over him.

The T-bird had dual exhausts, which gave it a nice, deep rumble. He drove carefully, cautiously. He had learned never to take chances, never to speed when he'd been drinking. Oh, he'd had an accident once. A broadside collision that had totaled his mother's Mustang, but it wasn't his fault. Okay, he'd had a few beers, but the other guy hadn't signaled. There were witnesses.

The bar at the pizza place, Lombardi's, was still open, which gave Weldon a chance to have a drink and assess his situation. He now had about forty dollars, his share of the shuffleboard winnings. He had spent the seventeen dollars left from his father's money. His father had expected him to use the fifty dollars to find a job.

"By the time we get back from Maui, I expect to find you gainfully employed," he had said. "Understand?"

His father. Weldon had never been able to understand why he was always so down on him. After all, he was his only son, and fathers were supposed to favor their sons, weren't they? But it was the other way around in their family. Laurie and

Denise were his pets, especially Laurie, who had won a scholarship to Minnesota. "Laurie's going to make Phi Beta Kappa," he was always saying, "and you can't get your ass through high school. Christ!"

But it wasn't his fault that he hadn't graduated; it was that dumb Mr. Montague, his English teacher. Okay, so he'd had six cuts, and the rule was that four unexcused absences and you could be flunked, regardless of your grade. But the decision to invoke the rule was left to the teacher. Montague could have passed him, *should* have passed him.

"I know why you skipped those classes, Yeager. You were in a hurry to get to the Purple Parrot."

Montague was a fine one to talk. Every Monday morning, he showed up red-eyed and with his hands trembling. It wasn't fair. It just wasn't fair. English had always been his best subject. He had started reading Hemingway in the ninth grade. He had read authors that Montague had never heard of. Montague was a shit.

"Your pizza's ready, fella," the bartender said.

The tab, including the drink, was twelve dollars, which meant he was now down to twenty-eight dollars, plus a couple of bucks in change. Not much, but what the hell, he would figure something out; he always had.

Driving back to the motel, the warm aroma of the pizza made him realize that he was hungrier than he'd thought. Spicy foods were the only ones he cared to eat when he was drinking: pizza, spaghetti, maybe a bowl of chili. He reached over to the glove compartment. It was there, a pint of Jack Daniel's, and it hadn't been opened. He and Rick would have a fine time, eating and drinking and talking, like in a college bull session. He wanted to learn more about that literary agent. His novel was just an idea at this point, a story about Livvie and Loon Lake, but now he would really get to work. He would stay in touch with Rick, send him a card at Christmas, maybe a note now and then. Rick would be a good friend.

But when he got back to the motel, Rick Wessell was sound asleep, his clothes lying in a pile on the floor.

"Hey, Rick, baby!"

Nothing.

He set the pizza and the bottle of Jack Daniel's on the dresser--the crummy room didn't have a coffeetable--and went to Rick's bed.

"Rick!"

He shook him. Nothing.

"Rick!"

He hollered in his ear. Nothing.

The nightstand had a radio built into it. Weldon turned it on and tuned in a rock station, turning the volume up as high as it would go.

Nothing.

He turned down the radio and stared at the sleeping form in disgust. The classic party had turned into a classic bummer. Rick Wessell, the Ivy League high-tech specialist, was out cold.

"I should've stayed at the Parrot," he said aloud.

He went to the dresser and got a slice of pizza. Then he opened the Jack Daniel's and took a long pull on it, gagging a little as he swallowed it; he didn't like the taste of straight whiskey. As he ate and drank, he wondered what he was going to do for the rest of the night. The room didn't even have a TV. He still had the keys to the T-bird, but it was nearly three o'clock; the bars would be closed.

He idly picked up Rick's clothes from the floor and shook them out. The label in the corduroy jacket caught his attention. *J. Press--New Haven, Cambridge, New York.* He checked the label in the chinos. *Brooks Brothers.* Rick Wessell wore classy clothes. He wondered what he would look like in them. What the hell, he would try them on--everything, shoes, socks, the works. Rick wouldn't mind, and it was something to do.

A rock tune that he liked was playing on the radio. Huey Lewis? Bob Seger? Sometimes he couldn't tell one group from another.

> *Goin' home to my darlin',*
> *Yeah, yeah, yeah,*
> *Never should've left.*

> *Goin' home where my heart is,*
> *Yeah, yeah, yeah,*
> *Leavin' on the next jet.*

As Weldon switched clothes, he sang along. *Goin' home to my darlin'*. He tossed his own clothes--cardigan, plaid cotton shirt, Haggar slacks, scuffed loafers--onto the other bed, next to his windbreaker. *Yeah, yeah, yeah*. Before putting on Rick's clothes, he took another pull on the bottle, Ah, the pause that refreshes! Maybe another one. Up to the lips and over the tongue, look out stomach, here she comes! Nice, very nice. He belched. *Goin' home where my heart is*. Rick's clothes were a pretty good fit. A little short in the leg and loose in the middle, but then Rick was shorter and heavier than he was. Hey, that would make a good rock 'n' roll song. *A little short in the leg/ And loose in the middle*. No, the other way. *Short in the middle boy/And loose in the leg/Yeah, yeah, yeah / Tune up your fiddle, boy/And let's tap a keg*. He broke into laughter and started doing a little dance.

"Hey, Rick, baby!" he hollered. "Get your ass outta that bed! I'm havin' a party!"

After putting on Rick's cordovan brogues (they were a little loose, but he could stuff them with Kleenex), he stood up to inspect himself. Nice, really nice. He smiled at himself in the mirror; he was proud of his teeth. Oh, he was a handsome dog; he really was. With a necktie, he would be very Ivy League-ish.

Yeah, yeah, yeah. He smoothed back his wavy blonde hair and ran his fingers over the fabric of the corduroy jacket. A nice soft texture.

"Nothin' but the best, huh, Rick?" he said. "You must be rollin' in bucks. Hey, speaking of bucks--"

He could feel Rick's wallet in an inside pocket. He took it out and rifled through the contents. A lot of cash--he didn't bother to count it--and several credit cards, American Express, VISA, Texaco, Sears, Shell. A guy could go a long way on those cards. A really long way--

He picked up Rick's gabardine topcoat from the chair and put it on. A little loose, but what the hell, that was the style, wasn't it? He slipped the bottle of Jack Daniel's into a pocket of the coat. Then quickly, purposefully, he gathered up his own clothes, making a bundle out of them with the windbreaker, and went to the door. *Goin' home to my darlin'.* He opened the door and went out.

He didn't look back.

> *I don't know why I did it. I'm lying here telling you about it, lying here in this strange hospital room, hurting--God, how I hurt!--but I just don't know. My life seemed at a dead end. I didn't like my life. I didn't like any of it, the Purple Parrot, Peggy Stipe in the back of a van, strawberry pop in the locker room. I was an embarrassment to my family, a macho phony to my friends. And maybe I saw a chance for a clean slate. Once upon a time, there had been haylofts and pine woods and blue herons soaring in the sun. Life had been fresh and true and lovely. Maybe it could be that way again. I don't know. I just don't know.*

Weldon eased the T-bird out of the motel parking lot and

turned left on Dempster, toward Springhurst. There was an important matter that he had to take care of at home. He still had that lovely second-wind feeling, but he was keenly aware that he was now driving a hot car. The slightest misjudgment would mean trouble. Bad trouble.

He turned on the radio. The car had a marvelous stereo with a tape deck. Next to the gearshift was a leather case containing a variety of cassettes, rock, jazz, folk, even the Boston Pops. He picked a cassette at random and slipped it into the deck. He lucked out: Peter, Paul and Mary, one of his favorites. *"Leavin' on a jet plane . . ."*

The music matched his mood. He was risking a return to Springhurst to retrieve his manuscripts, his stories and poems, and the retrieval would involve a small burglary--all because of that nerd Mr. Rozanski, the manager of the local Burger King.

The problem, in fact his whole damn lousy situation, had begun last month with a bank withdrawal, "the automatic teller caper," his dad had called it. But it wasn't a caper; it was a business transaction that went sour.

He had been low on cash (when wasn't he?) and needed a hundred bucks to repay some loans and finance his share of an important party that was coming up. He happened to discover that his father usually kept his card for the automatic teller in the glove compartment of his Impala, along with some other papers. The card was useless, of course, without the person's secret identification number. But when his father had first applied for the card, Weldon had overheard him telling Mrs. Yeager that he was going to use the last four digits of his social security number. He simply sneaked a look at one of his father's pay stubs, and he had the secret number.

One night, while his parents were watching *The Cosby Show,* Weldon told them that he was going to ride his bike over to Art Rothery's house. Instead, he got his father's card from the Impala, bicycled to a nearby branch of the bank, and was back in the house before *Cosby* was over.

He had never intended to *steal* the money; it was a loan that he would repay from his Burger King earnings before his father's bank statement arrived. Sure, his dad would wonder about a withdrawal and a deposit for which he had no slips. But he usually stopped for a couple a drinks on the way home from his office in the John Hancock Center; he would consider it an oversight.

It was a foolproof scheme, really, something to hold in reserve for future emergencies. But when he reported to work at Burger King one evening, after a few games of shuffleboard at the Parrot, Mr. Rozanski was waiting for him at the door.

"Don't bother to suit up, Yeager. You're through."

"But why?"

"I don't want you blowing your beer breath on our customers."

It was ridiculous! Weldon had seen Mr. Rozanski at the Purple Parrot so drunk he had practically fallen down. But there was no reasoning with the jerk. He was screwed--royally. First Montague, then Rozanski (and there had been a few others)-- there was a pattern to it. They were all jealous of him.

Because of Rozanski and his jealousy, the scheme came unraveled the day before his parents left for Hawaii. There was a terrible scene in the family room, his father ranting and raving, his mother crying.

"Junior, give me your key to this house," his father demanded. "You're not staying here while we're gone. You'll turn it into a goddamn discotheque--or worse."

His mother started to protest. "But, dear, don't you think that's a bit too--"

"Let me handle this, Louise. Pack a bag for him and call Phyllis Rothery. He can stay over there while we're gone. They've got plenty of room, and they owe us a few favors."

When Weldon went up to his room, they were still talking

about him. He could hear them through the register.

"Dear, do you think Junior might be an alcoholic?"

"My son an alcoholic? Don't be ridiculous."

"But I saw this program on TV--"

"Louise, drinking is a fact of life. He's got to learn to drink like a man, that's all."

As Weldon lay on his bedroom floor, listening, his ear pressed to the register, he laughed to himself. An alcoholic? What a laugh. Alcoholics were bums on some skid row, or the gray-faced men in business suits you saw slipping into Ben's Bar on Third Street at seven o'clock in the morning, having an eyeopener on their way to work.

Some people just didn't understand about alcohol. He wasn't a burnout. He didn't do drugs. He had tried marijuana once, but it had made him lethargic. Alcohol was different. It was, was--what was a good word? Enhancing? Yes, it enhanced his personality and his creative capabilities. It made him clever, witty, charming. Okay, so he'd overdone it a few times. What the hell, he was only eighteen. And he had been drinking for only a year. He was just a beginner. Give him a little time for crissake.

A siren!

Weldon tensed up. He was approaching Harlem Avenue and had spotted a red flasher light behind him, coming on fast. The police? For him? It couldn't be; not so soon. He slowed the car and pulled over to the side of the road. A fire truck roared by, stirring up a cloud of road dust.

"Whew!" he said aloud. "That mother was really traveling."

The sight of a red flasher light unnerved him. He'd better skip Springhurst. A T-bird with California plates cruising around town in the wee hours of the morning would invite a polite inquiry from the police. Also, in order to get into the house, he would have to smash out a basement window. Mr.

Peters next door, a light sleeper, might hear it. Besides, he'd memorized most of his stories and poems, the good ones, anyway. No, it was urgent to get the T-bird and himself out of the metropolitan area before an, an, what did they call it on TV?--an APB went out on him, an all-points bulletin. The Tri-State Tollway was just a few miles ahead. He would get on it and head south. He had no clear plan as yet, but a couple of drinks, and he would have everything figured out. But not on the Tollway; he didn't want to be spotted drinking at the wheel. A truck stop, maybe.

When he had been desperately trying to raise cash to cover that withdrawal, he had applied for a job, a dirty job, at a truck stop near Springhurst. His father might have given him credit for the effort, but no, get your ass out of here.

Still, he really wasn't too upset when his father packed him off to Art's house for two weeks. He had another key to the house that his parents didn't know about. They left for Hawaii on Sunday afternoon, driving to O'Hare airport in the Impala, which meant that his mother's new Escort was in the garage at home.

He knew that she kept a spare set of keys hidden in the trunk of all her cars (and the trunk door rigged so that it was always unlocked), in case she locked the other set in the car, which she frequently did.

On Monday afternoon, he stopped by the house to take the Escort to the Parrot--and discovered that the locks on all of the doors to house had been changed. He was stunned. How could that man have done such a cruel, insulting thing? And to his only son?

The following day, Art reported that Peggy Stipe had gotten a fake ID from the same print shop that had fixed them up. Peggy had been a year ahead of Weldon at Springhurst High and was now working for a local Realtor.

"She's gonna try out the ID at the Parrot tomorrow night,"

Art said. "Are you in?"

"Do fish like water?" Weldon said. Peggy had a reputation for being generous with her favors. "But you've got to loan me your van."

Siren!

Weldon didn't panic this time. He had left the Tollway and was now on the John F. Kennedy Expressway, in the far right lane, doing exactly fifty-five. A state police car flashed by. Traffic had been fairly light, but now it was getting heavier; maybe there had been an accident.

He had found a truck stop and tried out one of the credit cards. You could go around the world with somebody else's credit card; they never checked your signature. Rick's hand-writing was a small backhand, similar to his. If he practiced, he could fake it reasonably well. He had had a l'l snort in the men's room and then stopped at the cigarette counter for a supply of Certs and Clorets. It was time to start preparing. For what? Who could say? The successful crooks on TV were the ones who paid attention to details.

"You're a long way from home, aren'tcha," the attendant had said as he wiped the windshield. "How're things out in California?"

"Hectic," Weldon said. "As usual."

"Say, how's that new tax law you folks got workin' out?"

Weldon didn't know what he was talking about. "Like a charm," he replied, smiling. "They should've passed it years ago. Well, you take care now."

Flares!

There had been an accident, all right, but over in the northbound lanes. Weldon slowed as he passed it. Three cars, all badly damaged, one overturned. Flares, flasher lights, ambulances, wreckers. He speeded up and tried to put the disturbing scene out of his mind. It was a grim reminder of his own situation. He would have to drive the T-bird flawlessly;

40

even a fender-bender, and he would be finished.

He slipped a Bob Dylan cassette into the tape deck. He was on the South Side of Chicago now, 70th Street, 82nd, 87th. Coming up on 95th Street, he saw the sign.

I-94 MICHIGAN
LEFT 1 MILE

He smiled inwardly. *Goin' home to my darlin'*. He turned on the interior light and checked his supply of Jack Daniel's. Still two good drinks left. Some bar or liquor store should be open by six, surely in Calumet City, which was on the Indiana line. He would make it, thank you. *Yeah, yeah, yeah.* He would make it very nicely

BECKER: So you were tooling around the Chicago freeways at five o'clock in the morning, having yourself a ball? Trouble is, there are people like you on the roads everywhere. It's a wonder a patrol car didn't spot you sucking on that bottle.

YEAGER: I never drank at the wheel.

BECKER: Oh, yeah, I forgot. You did your guzzling at the truck stop. Which credit card did you use at that place?

YEAGER: The Texaco, I think.

BECKER: We'll know for sure when we check it out with Texaco and Shell. All right, you were on your merry way--did you have any particular destination?

YEAGER: Yes, sir. Beechers Grove.

BECKER: Your old hometown?

YEAGER: Yes, sir.

BECKER: But why Beechers Grove? I'd think some people would remember you from when you were a kid.

But that was the whole point, don't you see? To look up old friends, true friends, and relive the good old days.

Let me tell you about Beechers Grove. Coming in from Kalamazoo, you exit the freeway at Route 40, go north two miles and then turn left at Old Perch Road, which winds through the valley of the Paint Creek. Approaching the town, the road curves under a canopy of huge oak and maple trees that's like a tunnel of color in autumn. To the left is Great Oaks Farm, rolling green pastures, where they raise prize-winning Black Angus steers. At the entrance to the farm, there's a dairy store that sells fresh milk and eggs and butter. When I was a boy, they sold milk that came in quart bottles and had cream on the top. It was so rich, it left a mustache when you drank it.

Great Oaks borders the city limits, where there's a sign, in luminous lettering:

Welcome
BEECHERS GROVE
Pop. 17,476
A Family Town

On the corner of Old Perch and Main, there's a McDonald's, but I always preferred Bim's on Front Street, where you can get burgers on toasted buns and shakes with chunks of real ice cream floating in them. My mom took me there for a special treat the day I won a third-grade spelling bee. Bim made a big fuss over me. He's a great guy!

We lived just three blocks from Main Street, on Ludlow, opposite Cutler Park. That's where my buddies and I played some great football games, Bobby Wolf, Jack Gutmacher, Davey Farr, and whatever other guys that were available. They were just pickup games after school, two-handed touch or sometimes tackle, but, hey, they were like the Rose Bowl to us.

Afterward, we'd all troop over to my house, where my mom always had homemade cookies or cupcakes waiting for us. My mother didn't work then, and the house was usually filled with the smells of good things cooking or baking. One day, after an especially good game, Bobby Wolf had my mom prick our fingers with a needle, and we all took a blood oath to stay friends forever.

Beechers Grove. My town.

It's a town where kids walk to school. I had never ridden a school bus until my dad got transferred and we moved to Glenwood, a suburb of Dallas. The transfer meant a lot more money for him, but I was crushed. I had just won a short-story contest in my sixth-grade class at Hadfield School. Next summer, Livvie and I were planning to build a secret hideout, in the pine woods above the Narrows. I was filled with excitement, remembering what Livvie had said in the hayloft. And now, it was all falling apart.

"I know it upsets you to leave your friends, dear," my mother said. "But you'll make new ones in Texas."

They broke the news as I came into the kitchen after school one day. Laurie and Denise weren't home yet; they were trying out for the girls' basketball team. I wondered why my dad was home so early. I soon found out.

"But what about Loon Lake?" I protested.

My dad, who talks very fast when he is excited, gave me a cross look. "What d'you mean, 'What about Loon Lake?'" Even then, he was always mimicking me, always putting me down. "The cottage is going to be put up for sale, that's what."

"There's just no other way, dear--" my mother began.

"Let me handle this, Louise." My dad got a can of Coors

43

from the refrigerator. "Junior, it's over a thousand miles from Dallas to northern Michigan. What the hell d'you thing we're gonna do--commute?"

"No, but--"

"We can't afford the damn cottage, anyway. Laurie will be in college soon, then Denise, then you. Christ, we'll be tuition-poor for the next ten years."

And so my world collapsed. We went from a suburb of Dallas to a suburb of Kansas City to a suburb of Chicago. And through it all, there was a sameness to everything. The names of the towns--Glenwood, Brookdale, Springhurst. The names of the subdivisions--Quail Ridge, Spring Hill, Willow Wood. No Old Perch Roads canopied by trees; just freeways and congestion and angry drivers giving you the finger. No Bim's hamburgers, just Wendy's and Arby's and shakes with no ice cream in them. And worst of all, no Livvie.

I never saw Livvie again. We exchanged letters for a while, and I called her every few weeks. But the letters trailed off, and my dad complained about the phone bill. But Livvie and I didn't need phone calls or letters. We had a bond, an inde-structible bond. She was always in my heart. In the hayloft dream, which I dreamed often, she grew up. Her breasts filled out, and she became wonderfully passionate. *"Oh, yes, Weldon, do that."* Because of that dream, I knew that one day I would return--to Beechers Grove, to Loon Lake, to Livvie Buhl. It was meant to be. That's why--

BECKER: Hold it a minute, Yeager.

The telephone, which was on the bedside stand, was ringing. Lieutenant Becker turned off the tape recorder and picked up the phone.

"Becker . . . Yes, Nick . . . Uh-huh . . . When? . . ."

Weldon grabbed the trapeze and pulled himself up, frozen

in anxiety. Miss Wetherby sprang to her feet.

"Weldon! What's wrong?"

He ignored her. He knew what the call was about. One of the kids in Intensive Care had died. Oh, please, God, don't let it be Livvie.

"What about the other one? . . . Uh-huh . . . What does Doctor Glass think? . . . "

Miss Wetherby was leaning over the bed now, a look of alarm in her eyes. "Weldon?" she repeated.

"Well, give the prosecutor a call . . . "

If it was Livvie, he would get out of this bed somehow and dive through the window.

"Weldon, please lie back. You'll pull out the IV."

No, he would wait till he could write a note, a note about him and Livvie.

"I know it's Saturday, but he said he'll be there until we're finished. He wants the facts . . . "

They would find the note on his body, and there would be headlines in the papers about the star-crossed lovers.

"Okay, Nick, keep me posted. Any word on the game yet? . . . Well, buzz me if you hear anything. Thanks."

Lieutenant Becker hung up the phone and slowly turned to Weldon.

"Well, Yeager, it's now three counts of second-degree murder."

Weldon was so tense, he thought he was going to faint.

"W-was it the girl?" he asked.

"No, the Svoboda boy."

He let out a great sigh of relief and slumped back on the bed. "What about the girl?"

"She's on a thin string," Lieutenant Becker said. "But they're hopeful."

Miss Wetherby came around to the other side of the bed.

"Honestly, lieutenant," she said, "don't you think this is

enough for one day? This young man--"

Weldon reached out and touched her wrist.

"Please, Miss Wetherby," he said. "It's okay. I want to get it over with."

She took his left wrist to check his pulse. "I don't know, Weldon, this is just too much stress." She glanced at her wristwatch. "Your pulse is racing."

"We won't be much longer, nurse," the lieutenant said.

She drew a deep breath and sighed. "Well, it's against my better judgment, but-- How is your pain, Weldon?"

"Pretty bad."

"You'll require medication before you start again." She started to the door. "I'll get the cart."

Lieutenant Becker got to his feet and followed her. "I'll give you some privacy, Miss Wetherby."

"Thank you, lieutenant."

They left the room together, and Weldon found himself alone for a few minutes. The band was playing again at the football stadium. He looked out the window. Judging from the shadows cast by the trees on the ridge, he assumed that his room faced the west. He wondered where Intensive Care was. This appeared to be an older wing; Livvie was probably in a newer part of the hospital.

A thin string, Lieutenant Becker had said, but the doctors had hope. If there was any hope at all, Livvie would make it. He was sure of it. Livvie was strong and resourceful. Whenever they had explored the state forest on the eastern side of the lake, she had always marked a trail, so that they wouldn't get lost. And when they swam the Up Holly that time, she had finished fifty yards ahead of him and was ready to try swimming back.

Yes, Livvie would make it. He wondered if her parents were at the hospital. Probably; she was their only child. Henry and Lela Buhl would be near fifty by now, he figured. A tall, gaunt man, Henry Buhl had been one of the first farmers in the state to computerize his farming operations. Weldon had intended to seek his help in finding a job when he got to Loon Lake. Henry Buhl had liked him; so had Mrs. Buhl.

"You're a cut above those ruffians, Weldon," she had told him, the day some town kids picked on him at the harvest festival. "You just ignore them."

Lela Buhl was a stout woman, who always looked cool, even on the hottest day of summer. Weldon remembered her best standing on the landing at Buhl Farm, clanging an old iron triangle to signal Livvie home for supper. Sometimes Livvie was allowed to stay at the Yeagers' cottage for supper. She always helped with the dishes, and afterward, they would go down to the lake and skim rocks off the water, the air cool and misty and the lake quiet and still and shimmering in the twilight. They were such sweet moments! He wondered if---

"Weldon? . . . are you asleep?"

Miss Wetherby had returned with the medicine cart.

Weldon opened his eyes. "I wasn't sleeping," he said. "Just thinking."

She smiled. "Pleasant thoughts, I hope?"

"Uh-huh. About when I was a kid."

"Well, I've got something pleasant for your pain. Roll over a bit, please. There. That should hold you until this terrible inquisition is over."

She rearranged his gown and straightened his blanket. Weldon noticed streaks of gray in her hair. He wondered how old she was. Thirty-five? Forty?

"Your pain should subside soon," she said. "With an amputation, the first few days are the worst."

She reached to the IV stand to adjust the flow, eyeing Weldon with curiosity.

"You're bearing up quite well, Weldon," she said. "But you seem upset about something. I mean, something other than Lieutenant Becker and the charges against you."

47

Weldon looked at her apprehensively. "What do you mean?" he said.

"Well, I couldn't help but notice your concern about the Buhl girl in Intensive Care. Do you know her, Weldon?"

Weldon realized that if there were any chance of his seeing Livvie, Miss Wetherby would have to know. He steeled himself to make the effort.

"Uh, we . . . you see . . . uh, Livvie and I . . . "

"Take your time, Weldon."

"We grew up together . . . . We were, you know, *th*weethear*th*."

Miss Wetherby put a hand to her mouth. "Oh, dear God, Weldon!"

He told her the story, briefly, his voice barely audible.

"But didn't you know she was at Hillgrove?"

"No. I figured she was probably at State or the U. of M."

Martha Wetherby went to a window and stood there for a few moments, looking out in silence. When she came back to the bed, there were tears in her eyes.

"I've heard some tragic stories in this hospital," she said, "but I think yours is the worst. We do a good job of treating physical illness, but we can't do much about emotional anguish."

Weldon sensed an opportunity.

"You could do something about mine," he said.

"Like what, Weldon?"

"I'd like to tell Livvie I'm sorry. Could I go to Intensive Care to see her? You know, in a wheelchair or something?"

"You wouldn't need a wheelchair; I could wheel you there in your bed. Dr. Weng would have to approve, and Dr. Glass, our neurologist. And Lieutenant Becker, of course."

"How *ith* Livvie doing?"

"She hasn't regained consciousness, but Doctor Glass said he's seen patients with worse brain damage make a complete recovery."

Weldon was beginning to feel better. He was sure Dr. Weng would approve, and probably Dr. Glass. But what about Lieutenant Becker?

"Are her parents at the hospital?"

"Yes. They're staying at a nearby motel. The mother visits several times a day; the father drives down from their farm at night."

The door opened, and Lieutenant Becker came back into the room, a toothpick in his mouth.

"Your dietician took pity on me and gave me a snack," he said to Miss Wetherby. "Well, are we ready to resume?"

Miss Wetherby gave him a cool look. "Unfortunately, yes," she said.

"What about you, Yeager?"

"Ye*th, th*ir."

"Lieutenant," Miss Wetherby said, "before you begin, please let the record show that the patient's nurse strongly objects to the stress you're placing on her patient."

Lieutenant Becker, whose brown eyes had a deep, probing quality, folded his arms and looked at her for a moment.

"I'll do that, Miss Wetherby," he said. "And I'll also let the record show that the interrogating officer strongly objects to the stress your patient has placed on William Koehler, Marilyn Copple, Richard Svoboda, and Olivia Buhl."

Miss Wetherby didn't say anything. She turned, went to her chair, and sat down.

BECKER: Well, Yeager, when we left you, you were on your merry way. Did you go directly to Beechers Grove?

YEAGER: No, sir. I stopped at a couple of places.

BECKER: Such as?

YEAGER: A motel and a motor inn.

BECKER: For a drink, or to check in?

YEAGER: To check in.

BECKER: I'm confused again. You stole the car on Tuesday night. You were in Bridgton Thursday night. That leaves Wednesday. You mean you registered at two places on the same day?

YEAGER: Yes, sir.

BECKER: What were you doing, trying to find one with the best bar?

YEAGER: I wanted time to, you know, figure things out.

And he wanted time to inventory his new acquisitions--Rick Wessell's personal belongings. But first, it was imperative to replenish his supply of Jack Daniel's which he had polished off in a supermarket parking lot. He had left the freeway, reasoning that secondary roads would be safer in a hot car.

However, getting the whiskey had involved a close call. He had been making good time, much better that he had expected. As a result, when he arrived in Calumet City, the liquor stores weren't open yet; there would be a half-hour wait. He found a shopping center, where there was a liquor store next to an all-night drug store, and waited, listening to a Woody Guthrie cassette on the stereo.

He was parked directly in front of the liquor store; there were no other cars near him. As he was ejecting the cassette, he spotted a car with a flasher light mounted on the roof cruising his way. The driver was shining a spotlight into the various stores. He froze. A police car? A private security patrol? If it was the police, the California license plates would surely interest them.

He reached instinctively into the right pocket of his jacket for some Certs and began chewing them; hopefully, they would kill his breath. Did he have the registration for the T-bird? He didn't know. Did Rick keep it in his wallet? He hadn't noticed. He took the wallet from an inside jacket pocket to see. No, that wasn't Rick's wallet; it was his own. Oh, Jesus, he'd screwed up. His own wallet was supposed to be in a trouser pocket. Back at that truck stop, he must've gotten them reversed. But what good would the registration do, once they saw the photograph on Rick's driver's license? He should've smeared ink over the photo to obscure it, ink from a felt-tip pen, maybe. The car was getting closer. Oh, God, it *was* the police! Should he make a run for it? No, the drug store. Yes, that was it, the drug store.

Quickly, he opened the car door and got out, walking casually but purposefully toward the drug store. The patrol car passed by directly in front of him. Weldon smiled and waved to the officer; the officer, a young man with a mustache, smiled and waved back.

Inside the drug store, he went directly to a newspaper stand and picked up a copy of the *Chicago Tribune,* keeping an eye on the patrol car through the window. The car circled around, came up behind the T-bird, and stopped. Weldon could hear his heart beating in his ears. If only he had a drink. The officer was holding a microphone to his mouth and looking down at the T-bird's rear license plate. Weldon's knees were trembling. If an APB was out on him, it was all over--and before he had even gotten out of the state. God, why had he stopped here in the first place? But he knew why; the liquor stores in Indiana wouldn't open for another hour.

Wait! Was the officer putting down his mike? Yes. Now he was checking a clipboard . . . and now the patrol car was circling slowly around the other way and leaving the shopping center. All systems were go! Weldon was so excited, he wanted to cheer. He walked jauntily to the checkout counter and paid for the newspaper.

"Thank you, sir."

"Thank *you*, young man."

He hurried next door to the liquor store, which was now open, and bought two pints of Jack Daniel's, putting one under the passenger's seat, the other in the glove compartment. It was beginning to get light. There were now more cars in the parking lot. As a precaution, he moved the T-bird to the privacy of the service drive, behind a discount house. He took the pint of whiskey from under the seat, opened it, and took a long drink, leaning back in his seat to savor the warm, spreading glow. Ahhh! He felt very proud of himself. He had made all of the right moves--deciding to get out of the car, going into the drug store, and the smartest move of all, waving to the police officer. Oh, he was sharp, he was cool, he was ring-a-ding-doo. He took another drink.

"Thanks, fella," he said aloud. "I needed that."

An hour later, he was cruising down U.S. 12, on top of the world. He had stopped at a restaurant and eaten a good breakfast--corn flakes, bacon and eggs, and a double order of toast (he skipped the jelly, he never ate sweets when he was drinking). And then for the road, he had ordered a carryout of coffee (two cream, no sugar), which he spiked with a good jolt of Jack Daniel's, and was sipping now as he searched for a suitable motel, one where he could park the T-bird without the California plates being noticeable from the road.

The close call at the shopping center had been a lesson. Those damn California plates stood out like a sore thumb. The plates on most of the other cars on the road were much darker. The Illinois plates were blue; Indiana's were like a rainbow, with streaks of several colors; Michigan's were also blue (a couple of Michigan cars had been parked at the restaurant). But white? It was like waving a flag.

Then an idea hit him. If the T-Bird had only one plate, the rear one, it would protect him from being spotted by oncoming patrol cars, thus reducing his liability by fifty percent. Illinois cars had two plates, but he was in Indiana now, where they had only one. Also, the Michigan cars at the restaurant had had only one. The solution was obvious. When he found a motel, he would remove the front license plate. Hell, how many Indiana cops would know that a California car was supposed to have two plates?

Hey, that was good thinking, really good thinking. Details, that was the trick. Pay attention to even the tiniest detail. And anticipate. Anticipate the results of the most trifling decision, like deciding where to park. Every action has a reaction. He had learned that in physics. For every action, there is an equal and opposite reaction.

He hadn't particularly cared for physics, although he had liked his teacher, Mr. Bommarito, who had once played in a jazz combo. "Mr. B," as they had called him, had introduced him to really good music, jazz and country, rock and folk--older groups like Dave Brubeck and Herbie Mann; Merle Haggard and Hank Williams; Buddy Holly and the Everly Brothers; the Kingston Trio and Peter, Paul and Mary; and his favorite group of all, Simon & Garfunkel. He was playing the Peter, Paul and Mary cassette again when he spotted a perfect motel, a Best Western set well back from the road. He finished his spiked coffee, popped a few Certs into his mouth and turned into the long, curving driveway.

"Thank you, Rick, baby, wherever you are," he said aloud. "Thank you for the T-bird and the good music and the classy wardrobe. But most of all, thank you for being you, Rick, baby, you ring-a-ding-doo sweetheart. Oh, goin' home to my darlin', yeah, yeah--"

My second-wind feeling was holding beautifully. I felt like I could drink forever. Well, for a week or so, anyway. You think I'm putting you on? Hell, I'd done it several times. You see, I had learned that to be good for the long haul, a guy has to eat and sleep occasionally. It took me a while to learn that. When I first started drinking, I was like the other guys. I would go for long stretches without eating or sleeping and then heave my guts out. One night, after a wild party at Art's house (his parents were away), my mother heard me being sick in the bathroom and tapped on the door.

"Are you all right, dear?"

"Yeah, Mom. It must've been those chili peppers I had at Taco Bell."

"Oh, you poor dear. Take some of your father's Maalox. It's in the medicine cabinet, next to my Norform."

"Okay, Mom."

My dad always got a kick out of it, when I got sick like that.

"Junior," he once said, "when I was your age, I could chugalug a quart of beer. You just haven't got your sea legs yet."

But I was working at it. And I gradually learned that food and sleep are the keys to real staying power. Light meals, not heavy ones that ruin the glow; and short periods of sleep, just enough so that when you wake up, you've still got a good buzz on. Know what I mean? And then a quick eyeopener, and, hey, you're ring-a-ding-doo again, ready for the long haul.

And now, after four hours of sleep and a few eyeopeners at the Best Western (he had left a call), he was tooling down U.S. 20, with a plan, a foolproof plan. He knew exactly where he was going and what he was going to do.

All showered (with Dial) and shaved (with Rick's Norelco), his teeth vigorously brushed (with Crest), his mouth rinsed (with Scope), his underarms properly deodorized (with Ban), and his cheeks nicely patted with aftershave (Yardley)--he was ring-a-ding-doo again.

Oh, was he ever!

He was elated with the results of his inventory. He had retired the corduroy jacket and chinos, in favor of a navy blue blazer and gray flannel trousers, with a white oxford cloth button-down shirt and a red challis necktie. He saw a wonderful new life unfolding for him, a life that would be his fulfillment.

His new wardrobe was fabulous. He had everything--dress clothes, casual clothes; shirts and sweaters; socks and underwear; jeans and chinos; robe and pajamas; three more pairs of dress shoes, plus a pair of Weejuns loafers (which he was now wearing, liberally stuffed with toilet paper), even a pair of Reeboks that had hardly been worn. In the garment bags were two sport jackets, miscellaneous trousers, and four suits (one of them vested), all with that three-button Ivy League look.

But the wardrobe was just the beginning. In one cardboard box, he had found a little strongbox, unlocked, with various personal records, including Rick's birth certificate (it turned out he was twenty-three, not twenty-four), the car title, and--surprisingly--an envelope filled with snapshots of a nude woman on a bed (Rick's girlfriend?) in a variety of explicit poses. Looking at them, Weldon had become tumescent and taken them into the bathroom to relieve himself, letting his fantasies run riot. *"Don't stop, Weldon ... Please don't stop."* And then he had put the photos within easy reach for future therapy. Normally, he relied on a copy of Hustler for such therapy. But he had found the Hustler photographs rather gross; he had only a clinical interest in nude women with spurs and whips.

One of the letters in the strongbox had attracted Weldon's attention. It was on the letterhead of the Connecticut firm that had hired Rick.

> *... Thus, pursuant to our conversation of August 24, we are herewith pleased to offer you a three-year contract, with a starting salary of*

$125,000 a year, plus quarterly increases (to be negotiated). We have been impressed by your pioneering work at Helios and are confident that you will be instrumental in expanding the vocabulary of our X25j to 25,000 words or more.

Wow! A hundred and twenty-five thousand bucks a year, and he was only twenty-three. Rick Wessell, that sweet guy who couldn't hold his liquor, must be some kind of boy wonder. He had read about guys like that. The founder of one of the big companies (was it Apple?) was a multi-millionaire before he was thirty. Maybe Rick would be, too. Hell, with money like that, he could afford a dozen T-birds and have money to spare. And Brooks Brothers suits. And personal computers.

The computer was the really big item in the inventory, and it was going to be his salvation. It was in the trunk, a make and model he had seen advertised in *USA Today* and knew retailed for over four thousand dollars. It ought to bring at least half that amount on resale, which would finance a fairly good used car. He knew he couldn't drive a hot car indefinitely; he would have to get rid of it as soon as it had served its purpose.

But there were still problems. In order to register a used car, he would have to buy insurance. Also, he would need money to tide him over while he was selling the computer. And the plain fact was, he didn't have enough.

Rick's wallet had contained a little over two hundred dollars in cash. Added to his own twenty-eight dollars, that made about two hundred and forty. But he had dribbled away some of it on food and liquor, which meant he was down to about two hundred bucks. He had Rick's checkbook (there was a balance of over two thousand dollars in his account at a Santa Clara branch of the Bank of America), but it was useless to him. And so his only possibility was a cash advance of two or three hundred dollars on one of the credit cards, VISA or American

Express. And he wouldn't be able to get that kind of money at a Best Western; it would have to be one of the big hotels or motor inns, a Hilton, maybe, or a Marriott. He had found a AAA tour book in the glove compartment and thumbed through it. The nearest Marriott was in South Bend, but what had impressed him most was the full-page ad for an even bigger place in South Bend, the Briarwood Motor Inn. It had a very special look, like a rambling English Tudor manor, and AAA gave it its highest rating, four stars. Yes, that was for him. The University of Notre Dame was in South Bend. He might visit the campus and do some sightseeing. After all, being on the run was hard work. He deserved a little fun. He had phoned the Briarwood for a reservation.

> *"I'm sorry, Mr. Wessell, but we're booked solid. A big Junior Women's Federation convention. Uh, just a minute ... How long would it be for, sir?"*
>
> *"Just overnight. I'll be in town on business."*
> *"You're in luck. The computer shows that we've just had a one-day cancellation."*

And that's why he was tooling down U.S. 20 toward South Bend on a cool and crisp October afternoon, listening to the Rolling Stones on the stereo and reaching under the passenger seat for the Jack Daniel's---

Siren!

Quickly, he dropped the Jack Daniel's and glanced at the rearview mirror. Nothing behind him; it must be in the oncoming lane. Yes, a red flasher light was coming into sight over a little hill up ahead. But it wasn't the police; it was a paramedic unit. Whew!

But the mere sight of another red flasher light emphasized the increasing peril of his situation. Surely an APB was out on him by now. Time was running out, on both him and the T-bird.

That damn California license plate was like a beacon. After he got his own used car, he would have to get rid of the T-bird. The thought saddened him. It was a really neat car, and he had grown quite fond of it. He would probably end up with a crummy used Chevette, or something worse. And with his classy wardrobe? Shit.

Unfortunately, there was just no other option. Oh, after he got to Michigan, he could steal a license plate from some parked car. But that would be criminal. No, he would abandon the car in one of the larger cities, Traverse City or Cadillac, and take a bus back to Loon Lake. He would leave Rick his wallet and personal records, credit cards, everything like that (he would keep the snapshots) as evidence that he wasn't really a crook. He might even leave him the--

WAIT!

He had the title! He had the damn title to the T-bird! Where had he put it now? In the trunk? No, the strongbox was in one of those boxes in the backseat. With the title, he could *sell* the T-bird to himself, couldn't he? Or could he? He would have to find out. Oh, ring-a-ding-doo! He was so excited, he felt like he'd just won a million-dollar lottery. He needed a drink. He had to have a drink to figure this out. Not here in the car, but in a bar, where he could relax and do some serious thinking. *Goin' home to my darlin'/Yeah, yeah, yeah--*

He stopped at Swag's ("Have a Swig at Swag's"), a working man's bar on the outskirts of Rolling Prairie, and ordered a double Jack Daniel's and ginger ale. The bartender, an older man, asked for his ID.

"Can I see your driver's license, young man?"

It was the first time Weldon had been checked so far. He debated which driver's license to show him, his real one or Rick's. What the hell, he was on a good roll; he would try Rick's. He had smudged the photograph; now he would see if it worked.

58

"Yes, *sir*," he said, smiling. Without hesitation, he pulled out Rick's alligator wallet and handed the ID to the bartender, who gave it a quick glance and handed it back.

"I figured you was in your early twenties," he said. "I can tell a man's age within six months. Never miss. Now that was a double J.D. and ginger?"

"Right."

"You're a long ways from home fella, ain'tcha?"

"I'm on my way east to take a new job."

"Whereabouts?" The man served Weldon his drink.

"Connecticut."

"From California to Connecticut?" the bartender said. "That's life, I guess. We go where the jobs is. Well, enjoy your drink."

The place wasn't crowded yet; it was too early for the after-work crowd. Weldon took his drink to a table in the rear, near the phone booth. The title to the T-bird was in an inside pocket of his blazer. He took it out carefully, handling it as though it were gold, and studied it.

It was a pink slip, almost identical to the certificate of registration (he'd finally found that, in the glove compartment). The first thing he noticed was that Rick's signature wasn't on the title; there was only a computer printout of his name and address. The next thing he noticed was that there was no lien on the car. Apparently, Rick had either paid it off or bought the car for cash. (With his money, he could have afforded to.) To transfer the title, all that was required was the signature of the owner and the mileage on the odometer. There was no way of verifying the owner's signature, which meant that Weldon could sign Rick's name himself. Better yet, he could pay some guy at a bar to sign it. That way, the signature of the owner wouldn't be similar to his own when he applied for a new title.

BUT--and it was a big but--what if both the buyer and the owner were required to appear to complete the transaction? If they were, it was no go. How could he find out? In Illinois, the secretary of state handled motor vehicle business. Why not call the secretary of state's office in, in--oh, what the hell was the capital of Michigan? Lansing? Yes, that was it, Lansing. It wasn't four o'clock yet; their office should still be open. He made the call, courtesy of Rick's telephone credit card.

> *"No, Mr. Wessell, all that is required is that the buyer take the signed title to one of our branch offices and apply for a new title."*
>> *"What if it's an out-of-state title?"*
>> *"Makes no difference. A title is a title."*

He left the phone booth, smiling, and ordered another drink. It was all so easy! First, the credit card at the truck stop--no problem. Then the VISA card at the Best Western--no problem. Then the smudged driver's license here at Swag's--no problem. And now the title to an expensive automobile. It was ridiculously simple! Who said crime doesn't pay?--

BECKER: Yeager, I've got to hand it to you. You came close to perpetrating the perfect crime. Close, but not close enough. At present, there's no computerized system to verify signatures on motor vehicle titles. But there will be soon. Computers are taking over our lives. In five years, whenever you fart in church, a computer will log it and store the scent in its memory bank. So you had the title to Mr. Wessell's car and thought you were home free?

YEAGER: Yes, sir.

BECKER: And you probably would have been, if you hadn't turned down Campus Drive Thursday night. But I'm curious about the Briarwood. You actually stayed there?

60

YEAGER: Yes, sir.

BECKER: It's quite a place. My eldest son plays football at Notre Dame, but I could never afford the Briarwood on a policeman's salary. And you had it all for free. Was it worth it?

On looking back, Weldon realized that the Briarwood had been the beginning of the end. And he had had such high hopes. He had never stayed at a big hotel or motor inn before. When he was younger, his family had once made a trip to Disneyland, by way of the Grand Canyon, but they had stayed at ordinary motels. He had had to share a room with his sisters and sleep on a folding bed; Laurie and Denise always got preferred treatment.

And so the Briarwood, which was like a country club, was a wonderful new dimension for him. It wasn't just the nine-hole golf course, the indoor and outdoor swimming pools, it was the elegance of the place--the soft carpeting, the oak-paneled corridors, the crystal chandeliers in the lobby, and the way the employees made you feel special.

"It's a pleasure to have you with us, Mr. Wessell," the room clerk greeted him. "We hope you'll enjoy the Briarwood."

There were three restaurants and three bars, and you could sign your tabs and have them charged to your bill. Weldon, who was very hungry after the excitement over the title, ate in the main dining room, the Barclay Room. He sensed that it was not the proper atmosphere for spaghetti and Jack Daniel's, and so he ordered prime ribs and a split of sparkling Burgundy (he wasn't sure what a "split" was). The dinner rolls were fresh-baked; he ate four of them, with lots of butter.

Ah, this was the life, he thought as he leaned back in his chair and sipped his wine, surveying the crowd of well-dressed diners at the other tables. He blended in perfectly, he was sure.

He had changed into a suit, a black glen plaid, and was wearing black wing-tip oxfords. All of Rick's clothes fit him loosely, but this one seemed to be looser than the others. (Maybe Rick had been heavier when he bought this one.) He had wanted to punch an extra hole in his belt but couldn't find a sharp instrument. It didn't matter; if the trousers slipped down, he would put his hands in his pockets and hike them up. No one would notice. The wing-tips were also pretty loose; he had stuffed them with generous wads of Kleenex from the bathroom of his fourth-floor room, which had a marvelous view of the Notre Dame campus. He sighed contentedly. Yes, the Briarwood was special. When he was a famous author, he and Livvie would come here for a weekend. People at the other tables would whisper, *"That's Weldon Yeager, the famous author."* Livvie would be very proud of him.

After he left the Barclay Room, he checked out each of the three bars; he met Tina Rogers in the third one, Ye Olde Pub, which was very crowded, mostly with women--from the *JWF* convention, Weldon assumed. The bar was at the rear of the lounge, down a few steps. As he went by one table, a woman looked up at him and smiled. He smiled back, giving her the full effect of his teeth; his teeth were very sincere.

The bar was cleverly done, with rough-hewn beams and a planked floor. The seats at the bar were plush swivel chairs, backed by barrel staves. All of them were taken except one, but as Weldon started to sit down, he nearly crushed a *JWF* tote bag.

"Oh, I'm sorry," he apologized to the woman at his left. "Is this seat taken?"

The woman quickly grabbed the tote bag and set it on the floor.

"It is now," she said, giving him a big smile. She was an attractive woman, about twenty-five, Weldon guessed, with a frizzy hairdo, tinted silver, and a *JWF* convention button pinned to the lapel of her brown tweed suit--*Tina Rogers.* "Sit down, friend."

"Hey, thanks, Tina," he said, sitting down and signaling the bartender for his usual. "This is really nice of you."

"My ID button gives you an advantage," she said. "What's your name, friend?"

"I'm Weld--uh, I mean, Rick--" Oh, God, he had goofed. "Rick Yea--uh, I mean, Wessell. Rick Wessell."

Tina burst into laughter. "You're hilarious," she said. "You don't even know your own name." She turned to the two women she was sitting with. "Sue, Mary Lee--meet 'Mr. No Name.'"

They all laughed, and Weldon started laughing, too, to give himself time to figure a way out of this mess.

"No, I know who I am," he said. "I haven't had *that* much to drink. It's just that I've been reading this book by Chuck Yeager, you know, the pilot who broke the sound barrier? And I've got the name 'Yeager' on my brain."

"I can understand that," Tina said. "That man's had a remarkable career, hasn't he?"

Weldon had only read reviews of the book. "Has he ever," he said, and quickly changed the subject. "How's your convention going, Tina?"

"Marvelous. Simply marvelous. It's the best one we've ever had."

"What goes on at these conventions, anyway?" he asked her, steering the conversation away from himself.

"Oh, all kinds of things," Tina said. "Seminars on political and social issues, important speakers--"

"Like who?"

"Gloria Steinem was here yesterday."

"The feminist leader?"

"The same," Tina said. "And then we have all kinds of cultural events. We just came from a concert by a string quartet from Terre Haute--all women, of course--that played some marvelous Beethoven."

Weldon saw an opening.

"Say, do you know what Beethoven's doing in his grave?"

Tina looked puzzled. "No, what?"

"Decomposing."

She burst into laughter again. "Oh, you're fun-nee!" She slapped his arm playfully; her hand seemed to linger there for a bit. "Fun-nee, fun-nee, *fun*-nee!"

She took the last sip of her drink; she was drinking a martini. Weldon finished his own drink and signaled the bartender again.

"A round of substance, my good man," he said.

"A round of *what*?"

"Substance," Weldon repeated. "We want to abuse it."

The bartender didn't think it was funny, but Tina was giggling.

"And exactly what kind of substance do you want to abuse?" he asked them.

"Beefeater martini," Tina said, "with an anchovy olive."

"Jack Daniel's and ginger," Weldon said, "with lots of ice."

When they finished that drink, Weldon ordered another round. He had noticed that Tina was wearing a wedding band.

"Is your husband at the convention?" he asked her.

She made a face. "He's home jogging. He jogs five miles a day, rain or shine."

"Where's home?"

"Valparaiso. My husband frowns on us libbers. He's a male chauvinist."

"Seriously?"

"Uh-huh," she said, eating her olive. "And he frowns on martoonies." She giggled. "I mean, martinis. He's a health nut. He takes all kinds of vitamins and crap like that. I mean, it's r'diculous. He even talks about his stool at the breakfast table."

"His what?"

"His stool." She blushed. "You know, his bowel movements."

Now Weldon blushed. "I don't believe it," he said, laughing.

"Scout's honor." She raised her right hand. "I mean, he'll say, 'It was a bit too firm this morning. I'd better eat more fiber.' And then he'll start loading up on Granola or something like that."

Weldon got the picture: an attractive, liberated woman, neglected by her health-nut husband. Well, he had a remedy for that. He ordered another round and listened to her understandingly, drawing her out, asking the right questions. Gradually, the conversation got around to him.

"But if you're on your way t'Connecticut," she said, "what're you doin' in South Bend?"

"I stopped t'look up a girl I knew in college, but she's moved away."

"What school didja go to?"

"Yale."

"Really?" Tina was impressed. "Which college?"

Weldon didn't know what she meant; he thought Yale was just one big university. "Well, actually," he said, "I spent most of my time at the Bulldog Bar."

She laughed and started singing a song. "Bulldogs, Bulldogs, rah, rah, rah, Eli Yale--"

Was that the Yale fight song? Oh, God, had *she* gone to Yale? If she had, he was cooked. "Uh, did you go to Yale?" he asked her.

"No," she said. "P'due."

"Where?"

"*Pur-due.*"

He saw another opening.

"The Moilerbakers?"

She was puzzled again. "The *what*?"

"The Boilermakers."

This time she went into hysterics. "Oh, God, Rickie, you're s'funny, s'damn *fun-nee!*" Her knee was rubbing against his thigh. (Oh, he was witty; he was charming.) "How d'you say it, the Schmerlerbuckers?"

"No, the Schmoiler--uh, the Berler--Oh, shit, I f'rgit--get."

She was holding his hand now. (Oh, he was a Casanova.)

"What kind of work d'you do, Rickie, that makes you s'damn *fun-nee*?"

"High-tick. I mean, high-*tech*. What 'bout you?"

"Data processing."

He saw yet another opening and gave her a leering look.

"Lissen," he said, "wouldja care to process *my* data?"

She was stroking his thigh now. "Would I *ever*," she said.

(She was ready to fall into his arms.) "Your place or mine?" he asked her.

She leaned over and whispered into his ear. "Yours." She giggled. She was wearing a V-neck blouse; he could see her bra and cleavage. "What's yer room number?"

"Four-'leven."

"Why don'tcha run on up and get your--your data ready?" She giggled again. "Leave the door unlocked. I'll be up soon's I can get rid of Sue 'n' Mary Lee."

He grinned and winked. "Gotcha." He made a circle with his thumb and forefinger. "Don't fergit yer processor."

He got to his feet, unsteadily. After signing his tab and overtipping the bartender, he hiked up his trousers and started to leave. Going up the steps to the main level of the lounge, he stumbled, and his right shoe came off. He quickly slipped his foot back into it, but his heel caught on the counter and bent it down, with the result that the foot was half in and half out of the shoe. He continued on his way, unperturbed, limping slightly. Some women at one of the tables were looking at him and smiling. Or were they laughing? No, they couldn't be laughing. He was witty and charming. He was ring-a-ding-doo. They were probably admiring him. "Look at that handsome young executive!"

In the lobby, he sat down on a marble bench and put the shoe on properly. A bellhop was looking at him, curiously. The shoelace tied, Weldon stood up, hiked up his trousers again, straightened his tie, and walked with studied correctness to the elevator.

There was a smile of anticipation on his lips. The bright young executive was entertaining tonight.

A half-hour later, all was ready--he was ready, his room, which was a large one, with two double beds, was also ready. He had called room service and ordered a shaker of martinis. (He had left the Jack Daniel's in the T-bird; with three bars, plus room service, he didn't think he would need it.)

A gleaming silver tray was on the little breakfast table, which was next to the window--the martini shaker, two long-stemmed glasses, a little dish of anchovy olives, a silver bowl of peanuts, and some cocktail napkins. He was anxious to try a martini; he'd never had one before. But not now. No, he had to start pacing himself. It was going to be a long night. Tonight was going to make up for Peggy Stipe and all of his other failures. Tonight was going to be an *orgy*!

And he had prepared for it the way a proper lover should--brushing his teeth, rolling on some more Ban (even on his crotch), dabbing on some of the cologne he had found in one of the suitcases, putting on Rick's classy silk pajamas. They were maroon with white trim, a passionate color, he thought. (He wondered if Rick had worn them for the woman in the snap-shots.) They were monogrammed above the pocket, but he didn't intend to wear the top, just the bottoms. Hey, that would be a nice macho touch, him reclining on the bed in just those

67

pajama bottoms, with his "data" showing.

And that's how he was when the door opened and Tina, smiling seductively, came into the room.

"Ta, da!" she said, wiggling her hips and doing a little dance. "The processor has arrived!"

She set her purse on the dresser and gave him a greedy look. "Oh, wow!" Then she glanced around the room and whistled, drooling some spit on her chin. "Martoonies! And *data*!"

Weldon, grinning from ear to ear, started to sit up.

"No, you stay right there." She went to the bed and pushed him back against the pillows, giggling. "You c'n watch while I unwrap the processor." She giggled again.

"But don'tcha wanna martoonie?" Weldon asked her, loving all of this.

"Martoonies c'n wait." She kicked off her pumps. "Ah've gotta rush order on the *data*!" This time she laughed.

She undressed as if she were a strip tease artist, doing her little dance again, smiling at him, playing peek-a-boo as the clothes came off, singing some kind of song. It sounded familiar to Weldon--the "row your boat" song? Yes, it was. *Row, row, row your boat.* Her tweed jacket came off first, then her skirt, both of which she draped over the back of the upholstered chair, next to the dresser. *Gently down the stream.* Her white blouse was next and then her half-slip, which she tossed on the sawhorse, where the carpenters had been repairing the floor. *Merrily, merrily, merrily, merr-* She sat down on a bale of hay to take off her panty hose.

"Hey, be careful!" he warned her. "That hay is scratchy. It'll make a run in your hose."

"Oh, Weldon, it isn't *that* scratchy," she said, standing up and zipping her jeans. "Come on, let's go swimming or something, before my dad starts wondering what we're doing up here."

Weldon didn't want to go swimming; he didn't want

Livvie's scent to wash from his fingers.

"Let's hike up to the Narrows, instead," he suggested. "We haven't done that in a while."

"Okay," Livvie said, grabbing the knotted rope they had used to climb up to the loft. "Last one down's a rotten egg!"

They crawled through the barbed-wire fence at the bottom of the upper pasture. It was dense woods most of the way to the Narrows, hardwoods at first, and then great, towering pines that made them dizzy when they looked up at them. The pines kept the floor of the forest moist and cool and soft underfoot.

"Oh, I just love it back in here," Livvie said. "Don't you?"

"Yeah," Weldon said. "It's the best place of all."

Halfway to the Narrows, the forest opened on a sloping green meadow, where they usually stopped to rest. One time, they had packed a lunch and had a little picnic there. They flopped down in the soft meadow grass.

"Look, Weldon!" Livvie said, pointing up at the sky. "A blue heron."

Weldon scanned the sky, but saw no heron. "Where?" he said.

"Over there," Livvie said. "Follow my finger."

He rolled over and put his head next to her arm. Yes, he saw it now. The heron was up so high, he could barely make it out . . . soaring and gliding . . . soaring and gliding . . . soaring and gliding. The sun was hurting his eyes. He closed them and rubbed them . . . gently . . . merrily . . . life is but a dream . . . yeah, yeah, yeah . . .

Now his eyes seemed to be stuck shut. He wet a finger and wiped the crud from them. Slowly, they started to come open. But that damn sun was hurting them again. No, it wasn't the sun; it was the bulb in the lamp on the nightstand. Where the hell was he, anyway? Oh, yeah, the Briarwood. Where was-- what was her name? Tina? That was it, Tina. *TINA*! He sat up. His head ached violently, and his mouth tasted like there was glue in it. He looked over at the other bed; not even rumpled. He looked at the dresser; her purse was gone. Then he saw the message, scrawled on the mirror, in lipstick.

SOME DATA!

He groaned. Oh, God. Again. And this was going to be an orgy. He slumped back against the pillow. What time was it, anyway? He didn't own a wristwatch; he had hocked it. The drapes were still drawn, but he could see that it was daylight. He picked up the phone. "Wouldja please gimme the c'rrect time?" His voice sounded raspy, and his tongue was thick. "Seventen? Thank you." Good God, it was after seven already! He had to get cutting. Today was the big day, cash-advance day.

He forced himself to sit up. His head was about to explode; pain cut across his forehead like a knife. He had blown it. He had lost his second wind. No quick nap, that heavy meal in the Barclay Room--he had violated his own rules.

He needed a drink, urgently. He shouldn't have left the Jack Daniel's in the car; Jack Daniel's was his mother's milk. But the martini shaker was still there. He had ordered enough for three drinks each. Had Tina drunk it all? It was probably stale by now, but it was still alcohol, wasn't it?

The breakfast table was to the right of his bed. He rolled over and started to stand up, his head pounding like a sledgehammer. His knees were wobbly. When he tried to take a step, he keeled to one side, hitting a chair. Bracing himself against the table, he lifted the lid of the shaker. He was saved! There was still a lot in it.

With trembling hands, he filled one of the long-stemmed glasses, sloshing a bit over the side. His hands were shaking so badly, he had to use both of them to lift the glass to his lips. He took a swallow and immediately began to cough and gag. The glass fell from his hands and hit the silver tray, shattering. God, that was vile stuff!

He started to throw up and put his hands over his mouth, but nothing came up. He fell to his knees, retching--retching so fiercely, he thought his intestines would come up. The bathroom. He had to get to the damn bathroom. He crawled there on his hands and knees, still retching. The drawstring of his passionate pajamas came untied; they slipped down to his knees.

The bathroom door was closed. He reached up for the knob, missing it several times before he finally got the door open. He flung himself over the toilet bowl, retching convulsively. He knew what his problem was: the dry heaves. He had heard of them, but had never had them. Stumblebums and alcoholics got the dry heaves, not people like him. This was just a slight case of misjudgment.

The constant retching had placed great pressure on his bladder, and he began to urinate--on the floor. He tried to stand up and direct the stream into the toilet, but as he did so, he lost control of his bowels. Diarrhetic stool gushed down his legs and onto his pajamas, which were now around his ankles. As he turned around to sit down on the toilet, he tripped on the pajamas and fell down. Urine and liquid stool splattered the floor and one of the bathroom walls.

As he lay there, retching, he was convinced that he was about to die. So this is how it ended, he thought--wallowing in his own shit in the Briarwood. Ring-a-ding-*splat.*

But he didn't die. His problem ran its course. He regained control of his bowels and bladder, and the retching slowly subsided. His heart was still pounding, and he was breathing heavily, but he had survived. Oh, if he only had some cold beer. The martinis! He had to get some of that gin into his system--somehow. He cleaned up the mess as best he could, using bath towels soaked in hot water (the maroon pajamas were ruined; he tossed them into the wastebasket). Then, naked and with his whole body trembling, he staggered to the breakfast table. As he leaned over to get the martini shaker, he broke wind. Some remaining liquid stool squirted out and stained the bedspread. He ignored it and took the shaker back to the bathroom.

His hands were shaking so badly, he poured some of the martini into a bathroom tumbler, diluting it with water. The stuff still tasted ugly, but he was able to hold it down. Then a little more, and a little more--

An hour later--all shaved and showered and wearing a gray sharkskin suit (no more glen plaid for him!) and the cordovan brogues (or wing-tips, either!)--he picked up the phone.

"This is Mr. Wessell in four-eleven. Would you please have them bring my car around?" (The Briarwood had valet parking.) "And send a man up for my bags, please. I'm checking out. . . Yes, four-eleven. Thank you so much."

There were three others ahead of him in the checkout line. The wait gave him time to review his options. Be calm, be cool, be collected, he told himself, but his heart was racing, and he was breathing rather rapidly. Did it show? He would use the American Express card, he had decided; the ads said that was the one preferred by business executives. The line moved up one person. The first thing the cashier would do--an attractive young woman was handling this line-- would be to run the credit card through a computer terminal. If it was rejected as a stolen card, what would he do then? Laugh about it? Yes, that was it. Humor always disarmed people.

"You mean my secretary screwed up again?" he would say. "I *told* her. You see, our offices were burglarized last week, and I thought that card was stolen. But I found it a couple of days later and *told* her to notify AmEx, but--"

The line moved up another person.

If they didn't buy that story, what then? He could ask them to accept a personal check. But he hadn't had a chance to practice writing Rick's signature, and the smudge over the photograph on the driver's license might make them suspicious--

"Next."

He stepped forward and gave the woman his best smile. "Good morning," he said, cheerfully. "Wessell, four-eleven."

She smiled back. "Good morning, Mr. Wessell," she said. "Looks like another marvelous day."

"Doesn't it, though?" he said. "Indian Summer, almost."

She turned to a machine and pressed a few buttons. A print-out rolled out of the machine.

"Let's see now," she said. "Room, ninety-two fifty. Restaurant, thirty-seven ninety-eight. Bar, sixty-two fifty. Room service, thirty-three forty-six. That's two hundred twenty-six forty-four. Plus ten percent tax, twenty-two sixty-four, for a total of two hundred forty-nine oh-eight. Is there anything else, sir?"

This was the moment. His stomach was growling. Oh, God, was he going to fart?

"Well, actually, I'm running a little low on cash. Could you let me have an advance on my AmEx card?"

"We certainly can," she said. "How much will you need, Mr. Wessell?"

"Three hundred?"

"Are you sure that will be enough? You can go to five hundred, if you wish."

A bonanza! But play it cool; don't appear eager. "Wel-l," he said, pretending to think the matter over. "Maybe I should. You know how cash dribbles away these days."

"Do I ever?" She smiled again. "And how would you like that, sir? Large bills or small?"

"Twenties and fifties, please."

She took the AmEx card and moved to her left, where Weldon couldn't see her. That's where the computer terminal would be. He held his breath. Then she reappeared, talking with another person, a man, and pointing to Weldon. The two of them went through a door next to a file cabinet. Weldon's heart was pounding. The woman came out in a moment, with a little green folder in her hand, and went directly to Weldon.

"I'm afraid there's a slight problem, Mr. Wessell." His heart was about to burst. Should he make a run for it? "The Brink's truck hasn't arrived yet, and so we're low on twenties and fifties at the moment." She opened the folder and took out some bills. "I'm terribly sorry, sir, but the best I can do right now is three hundreds and four fifties."

Weldon looked at the bills and feigned a frown. "Are they all legal tender?" he said.

She laughed. "They certainly are, sir," she said. "Guaranteed."

He gave her another smile, and the rest of it was routine. She didn't even compare his signature with the one on the back of the credit card, which didn't surprise him. So far, no one had.

"Here you go, Mr. Wessell," she said, handing him his receipt and the AmEx card. "Thank you for being our guest at the Briarwood. Please come back soon."

"Oh, I will," Weldon said, giving her a final smile. "This is without doubt the finest place I've ever stayed at."

And it was, he thought, as he turned and started across the lobby, a new spring in his step. The dry heaves were a distant memory. He was ring-a-ding-doo again! He wondered if one of the bars was open yet. No, he didn't want that attractive cashier to see him heading for a bar this early. It would spoil his bright-young-executive image.

"Mr. Wessell?" It was the bellhop. "Your car's ready, sir, and your bags are in the backseat."

"Thank you," Weldon said, tipping the man five dollars.

"Thank *you*, sir," the bellhop said. "Have a good trip."

BECKER: What time did you check out of the Briarwood?

YEAGER: About nine-fifteen.

74

BECKER: You lucked out. A stolen-card report was fed into the computer at nine-forty. Mr. Wessell was so busy piecing his life together, he forgot about the cards until then. You left him in a hell of a mess--no toothbrush, no razor, no shoes, nothing. The manager of the motel was suspicious. He thought Wessell was a gay who'd been rolled.

YEAGER: But he said he had friends in Chicago.

BECKER: Not close ones, and you don't call up acquaintances when you're stranded in a motel room with nothing to your name but your underwear.

YEAGER: What did he do?

BECKER: Called the police first. And then he made a collect call to his father in Boston. His father flew out to Chicago, but all of that took time. The motel manager loaned him a jogging suit, and the father took him around to the stores and bought him clothes and personal articles. They didn't get out of Chicago until Wednesday.

YEAGER: Did he report to his new job okay?

BECKER: Barely. It was a hassle getting him a driver's license. Meantime, you were having yourself a fine time with his California license. How did you manage to use it as an ID?

YEAGER: I smudged ink over the photograph. A Magic Marker.

BECKER: No wonder merchants get swindled. They beg for it. How many more times did you use those cards?

YEAGER: I don't know. Six, maybe.

BECKER: At bars, I suppose?

YEAGER: And a gas station.

BECKER: Texaco?

YEAGER: No, Shell.

BECKER: Are you sure?

YEAGER: Yes, sir.

He was sure because it was near the Notre Dame campus, and the station had a big green sign above the pumps. *GO IRISH Byers Shell.*

The station was across the street from McGinty's, the college hangout where he ate lunch (he was trying to get back his second wind). It was a marvelous place that served beer in big steins and charcoal-grilled bratwurst on long, hard buns that crunched when you bit into them. One wall was filled with framed pictures of Notre Dame football greats, even the "Gipper."

It was the kind of college hangout that Weldon had always dreamed of. But for some reason that he couldn't define, he felt oddly out of place. It wasn't just his clothes, his three-button suit and striped tie; it was something more, something deeper. It seemed crazy, but he felt *older* than the others. Which was absurd, really; he was younger than most of them. But even so, he felt more mature. And the others seemed to regard him that way. One person, a guy in a *Fighting Irish* sweatshirt, asked if he was on the faculty, thinking he was an instructor on his lunch break. And Weldon wondered: Had the role he'd been playing actually changed him? Was he becoming what he was pretending?

It still bothered him when he left McGinty's for a stroll around the campus, only in a different way. He had always loved college campuses. Ever since he was a boy, he had believed that one day he would be a student at some wonderful university. And he would be, this very minute, if Mr. Montague and a few others hadn't conspired against him. But now--was he beyond college? Had he burned that bridge, too?

Well, what the hell. Authors didn't really need college. Ernest Hemingway had never gone to college, and he had won the Nobel Prize. Authors lived colorful, adventurous lives-- some of them, anyway--and drew their stories from those experiences. He was on a colorful adventure right now, wasn't he? Maybe one day he would write about it (leaving out the chapter on the dry heaves, of course). But the chapter on Beechers Grove, the next stop on his itinerary, would be a good one, a very good one--the loyal hero looking up his boyhood chums, his blood brothers.

The thought cheered him up, and he started back to the T-bird at a brisk pace, anxious to get on with it. Less than a hundred miles to Beechers Grove now, a nice leisurely drive, with an occasional stop along the way.

But the leisurely drive almost turned into a disaster. He had just crossed the state line, on a secondary road, doing exactly fifty-five, the posted speed limit, and listening to a Boston Pops cassette on the stereo. It was a beautiful, sunny day, but dark clouds were showing on the western horizon, and he wondered if rain was moving in.

As he was enjoying a Strauss waltz, an oncoming patrol car passed by. That was the fifth one since the Best Western, and each time he had congratulated himself on his foresight in removing the front license plate.

"Take another bow, Weldon, baby," he said aloud. "Those

dumb cops'll never catch you. Yeah, yeah, yeah."

He was coming over a small hill, when--Oh, my God! He jammed on the brakes. A farmer on a tractor was just ahead of him, poking along at about ten miles an hour. He couldn't swing around him; it was a two-lane road, and a big truck was barreling his way. The T-bird's tires screeched, and the car started to skid. But Weldon fought it, managed to miss the tractor, and brought the car to a stop near the edge of a deep ditch.

"Son-of-a-bitch!" he muttered.

His heart was racing again, and his hands were shaking. What a way for his colorful adventure to end, he thought, running down some dumb farmer on a tractor. He unfastened his seat belt, lowered his window, and leaned out.

"You goddamn farmer!" he shouted, giving him the finger.

But the farmer kept poking along and turned into the driveway of a farmhouse. Weldon wanted to go after him and ream him out, but there were cars behind him now. He backed the T-bird onto the highway and got going. As he was picking up speed, he reached for his seat belt. Illinois had a seat-belt law, but he wasn't sure about Indiana or Michigan, and so he had stayed buckled up all the way. Another dumb way for his adventure to end, to be stopped for a seat-belt violation. Details, be thought smugly, he was paying attention to details.

The near-miss had shaken him up so badly, he stopped at the next two bars to calm himself, ordering a double Jack Daniel's at each. At the first one--

YEAGER: I have to go to the toilet. You know, a bowel movement.

Lieutenant Becker turned off the tape recorder. Martha Wetherby had already come around to the other side of the bed and was getting a bedpan from the lower shelf of the bedside stand.

"If you'll please excuse us, lieutenant," she said.

"Gladly." Lieutenant Becker was on his way to the door. "I'll be out in the hall."

Miss Wetherby removed the plastic cover from the bedpan.

"Weldon, grab the trapeze, please, and lift yourself up. That's it. Now grab the guard rail with your left hand, but be careful of the IV. Wait, your oxygen tube is getting tangled. There. That's better."

She lifted Weldon's gown and slipped the bedpan under him. It was the first time he had seen the catheter that was inserted into his penis. Tubes, he thought. He was a creature of tubes.

"Thi*th* is so embarra*th*ing," he said.

"Don't feel that way, Weldon. It's a perfectly natural function."

"Not this way."

"I've had patients who weren't able to use a bedpan," she said, "so count your blessings."

Slowly, Weldon settled himself on the pan. At least it was more sanitary than the bathroom at the Briarwood, he thought.

"What do I do now?" he asked her. "Just go?"

"That's right. Do your regular number. Here's the tissue." She went to the door. "I'll give you some privacy, Weldon, but if you need help, holler. I'll hear you."

Weldon used the bedpan abundantly, noisily, and the odor was foul. Some loud, booing noises were coming from the stadium. The crowd was probably protesting a referee's decision. He could picture the scene in his mind's eye. There would be pompoms and pennants and cheerleaders in short skirts. Afterward, there would be wonderful parties. He wondered if Livvie had ever been a cheerleader. She would make a good one. She had the enthusiasm and the agility. Once, when they were climbing trees in the state forest, she had---

"All finished, Weldon?" Miss Wetherby had come back into the room.

"Yes, ma'am."

"Lift up again, please. That's it."

She took the bedpan to the bathroom. Weldon could hear the toilet flushing. She returned with a can of air freshener, which she sprayed around the room. She opened another one of the windows and then went to the call box.

"Martha in four-oh-four, Bernice. Please tell Lieutenant Becker that we're ready for him."

When Lieutenant Becker came back into the room, he seemed to be looking at Weldon with new interest.

"Yeager," he said as he sat down, "Miss Wetherby told me about you and the Buhl girl."

Weldon grew tense. Was this more bad news?

"Did your family have a cottage at Loon Lake?"

"Yes, sir."

"Upper arm or lower?"

"Lower."

He smiled slightly and tilted back in his chair.

"Well, I'll be damned," he said. "I caught the finest bass of my life in the lower arm of Loon Lake. There aren't many cottages on the lower arm. It's mostly state land. But I remember one place that had a silver flagpole with a bed of marigolds around it."

"That was our place."

"And on the other side of the lake, there was a farm with a green barn."

"Buhl Farm," Weldon said.

The lieutenant started picking lint from his trousers.

"I was going to buy some property on the lower arm, but folks got kind of nervous. Complained that property values would drop. Of course, that was years back, when things weren't too liberal."

He folded his arms and crossed his legs.

"Well, Yeager, I'll not add to your troubles." He turned to Miss Wetherby. "Nurse, Yeager has my permission to visit the Buhl girl in Intensive Care, when and if the hospital approves. Just one visit, understand?"

"Yes, lieutenant." Miss Wetherby was looking at Weldon, smiling.

"I'll leave a standing order at the nurses' station. You can show it to whichever officer is on duty."

Weldon felt like crying. For the first time since he had opened his eyes today, something good had happened. A profound feeling of gratitude welled up in him, gratitude to this tall, stern lieutenant with the dark, probing eyes.

"Thank you, sir," he said. "You're very kind."

Lieutenant Becker gave him a hard look.

"Don't push it, Yeager," he said, reaching for the tape recorder. "Don't push it."

BECKER: All right, Yeager, let's see if we can wrap this up before the game's over.

YEAGER: Yes, sir.

BECKER: So you were on your way to Beechers Grove, still living it up on those credit cards. By the way, you lucked out again. The smaller establishments wouldn't have computer terminals. They rely on lists the companies mail out.

Weldon was aware of that. One summer, he had worked at a nursery in Springhurst and had handled a lot of credit-card sales. He also knew--or thought he knew--why clerks were careless in checking signatures. They preferred to avoid a confrontation. It took courage to say, "I'm sorry, sir, but this isn't the signature on the card." And as long as the card wasn't on the list of bad numbers, what difference did it make? The credit-card company, not the store, would be stuck.

BECKER: Well, Yeager, was it an exciting homecoming?

Weldon had hoped it would be--oh, how he had hoped!--and he had made careful preparations. He knew that Bobby, Jack, and Davey would be put off by his three-button suit. What was their old buddy Weldon doing in clothes like that? And so before he left the last bar he stopped at after the tractor incident, he changed clothes, in the car, putting on the corduroy jacket and loafers and taking off his tie.

He also knew that his friends would wonder, maybe even be suspicious, about the California license plate. How would he explain it? He couldn't, and so he would park the T-bird in a safe place while he was in Beechers Grove and rent a car. That is, *if* Bobby, Jack, and Davey were at home. They might all be away at college. But that was no problem. He would still have a good visit and then drive down for a reunion later, maybe over the Christmas holidays. He might even bring Livvie. She would remember them; he had often talked about them at Loon Lake.

All the way to Michigan, a sense of excitement mounted in him. His homecoming was going to be an event, an important event. Turning onto Old Perch Road, he began planning his visit. He would have a burger and fries at Bim's. Should he have one of those marvelous shakes, too? Better not; too sweet. Hey, he could ask the people who now lived in their old house on Ludlow if he could see his old bedroom. No, too risky; they would smell liquor on his breath and be suspicious.

But he could drive by Hadfield School and maybe stop and look up his old sixth-grade teacher, Miss Doebler. She was the one who had called him in after the judging in the Young

Authors contest and said, "Weldon, you're a writer. You've got real talent." No, he'd better not do that, either; she would catch a whiff of his breath. But he could call her up after she got home. Yes, that was the thing to do. He would tell her--what would he tell her? That he was enrolled in the Writers' Workshop at the University of Iowa, and that she had been right--he was going to be an author. "I couldn't have done it without your help and encouragement," he would say. She would be very proud and brag about him to the other teachers.

But as he approached Beechers Grove, he could scarcely believe his eyes. There was no tunnel of color canopied by trees; there were no trees. Old Perch Road was now a bustling five-lane highway, with fast-food places everywhere. The city limits had been expanded, and there was now a new sign.

BEECHERS GROVE
Pop. 32,504
The City of Tomorrow--Today

There was no Great Oaks Farm; it was now Great Oaks Mall. And the rolling green pastures were now a condominium development. He had been prepared for growth, but *this?* And then he saw the reason for it, a complex of low, rambling buildings that looked like laboratories.

GMC ROBOTICS
World Headquarters

The older part of the town was relatively unchanged, but Bim's was gone, replaced by a Baskin-Robbins ice cream place. (He decided to skip the burger; he could get a hamburger at a McDonald's anywhere.) And there was a new apartment complex on Ludlow.

He drove up Ludlow twice. Their old house had been

painted white with green trim when they lived there; it was now gray with black trim, and there was no vegetable garden in the backyard. His father had been an avid gardener, but when they moved to Texas, he gave it up. The climate was too hot and dry, he said, and he had more important things to do.

Ludlow was still a lovely street. In late fall, it would be ankle-deep in leaves, and with the first snowfall of winter, it would look like a fairyland. He remembered one Christmas when the neighborhood children had gone caroling up and down Ludlow. It had been so lovely, the snow clinging to the trees, and the houses all lit up with yule displays. People had waved to them from the windows and come out on the porches.

"Merry Christmas!" they had called to the carolers.

He was ready for a drink, and it was time to start making phone calls. He decided on the Paint Creek Bar on Fourth Street, one of his father's favorite spots, which had parking in the rear. To be extra safe, he backed the T-bird into a space next to the building, so that the California plate couldn't be seen. (Anticipate, anticipate!)

He ordered his usual and then thumbed through the phone book. There was no listing for a Robert Wolf on Pine Street (Bobby was a junior, too); they had probably moved away. The Farrs still lived on McCall Street, but when he called, he learned that Davey was away at college, Ohio State. Damn! He was striking out. But he scored with the Gutmachers.

"Hello, is Jack in, please?"

"Yes, he is. Just a minute, please. . . . Hello?"

"Jack, ol' buddy. Weldon."

"Weldon? Weldon who?"

"Weldon Yeager."

"Do I know you from somewhere, Weldon?"

"We were classmates in grade school."

"Hadfield?"

"Yeah."

"Weldon *Yea*ger? No, I don't recall a--"

He didn't remember him. His blood brother didn't remember him.

"Sorry, fella, I must have the wrong Gutmacher."

He slammed down the receiver. Son-of-a-bitch! Tight-lipped, he went back to the bar and ordered another drink.

"That was Jack Daniel's and ginger ale, wasn't it?"

"Yeah. Make it a double this time."

He finished the drink quickly and then went across the street to a liquor store, where he bought two pints of whiskey. Beechers Grove was no good anymore. Why the hell had he come back here, anyway? The town was down the tube. Everyplace was down the tube--except Loon Lake. Towns like Loon Lake never changed; people like Livvie Buhl never changed.

He hurried back to the T-bird. He would take the freeway, he decided. There would be no problem. It would be dark most of the way, and he could have an occasional snort at the wheel, so long as the cars behind him weren't too close. He cruised slowly up Fourth Street and turned left at Old Perch Road. At the city limits, he remembered that he hadn't gone by Hadfield School. To hell with Hadfield ; it had probably been torn down. To hell with Miss Doebler; she probably wouldn't remember him, either. He began to pick up speed. *Goin' home to my darlin'/Yeah, yeah, yeah--*

BECKER: But if you were heading for Loon Lake, Yeager, how the hell did you end up in Bridgton?

YEAGER: I wanted to, you know, rest a little.

BECKER: And drink a little?

YEAGER: Yes, sir.

85

BECKER: What bar did you stop at?

YEAGER: I don't remember the name.

BECKER: Think hard. It will come to you.

It had started to rain, not a hard rain, but a sort of drizzling mist. But he still made good time, and the long drive gave him time to review his plans.

His top priority, of course, was obtaining legal ownership of the T-bird. He would have to apply for a new title, but did he want to do that in Loon Lake, or should he go to some neighboring town? Why not Loon Lake? So he arrives one day with a California plate and a day or two later has a Michigan plate. So what? It's all perfectly legal. Anyone who asks, he'll tell them the truth--that he just bought the car (he won't tell them how much he paid) but hasn't registered it yet.

And then with the T-bird legally in his name--the computer. He might have to run an ad in a big-city newspaper, but that was no problem; with the five hundred dollars from the Briarwood, he had a nice cash cushion. And if he really got in a bind, he could always sell the T-bird and buy a cheaper car. He would probably net several thousand dollars from the deal. With money like that, he could-- Hey, he could start playing the stock market! Why not? He read the *Wall Street Journal* occasionally; he knew a little bit about stocks and bonds. And what he didn't know, he could easily learn from books. Why, he could parlay a few thousand bucks into a fortune. Oh ring-a-ding-doo! He had to stop somewhere and really think this over. This changed his whole game plan.

That's when he saw the sign.

BRIDGTON
(Hillgrove College)
EXIT 1 MILE

86

He lost his bearings, trying to find a bar with suitable parking arrangements, but he found a good one--a rustic kind of place, similar to the Purple Parrot. The sign out front was a big revolving jug. (Hey, that was the name! The Brown Jug.)

That's were he met Stan and Eddie, two real nice guys, about his (Rick's) age, who knew a lot about college football and loved to argue. The three of them had several rounds, debating who would win the Big Ten championship this year, Michigan or Ohio State.

Weldon bought all of the drinks; he even set up a round for the house, and the place was very crowded. (What the hell, it was his last fling with the credit cards.) They were still arguing when Weldon got ready to leave.

"Well, ah don't care what you guys say," he said. "Mishagun's gonna take it. They got the best d'fense."

"Hey, Rickie, you can't leave without lettin' us buy a round," Stan said.

"Yeah," Eddie agreed. "It ain't fair."

Weldon grinned. "Twist m'arm," he said.

They did, and Stan signaled for another round.

"Lissen, you guys," Weldon said as he finished his drink. "How the hell do I get back on the fr'way?"

"Simple," Eddie said. "You go this way"--he pointed-- "'bout two miles, then turn left at the amber light."

"Naw, that way's no good," Stan protested. "It goes by the college."

"But it's the shortest," Eddie insisted.

"And the slowest," Stan said. "F'rget the amber light, Rick. Keep goin' to the first stop light, turn left, then follow the signs. Nothin' to it."

"Okay, guys," Weldon said, standing up. "Y'all take care now."

"You, too, Rickie."

"Yeah, Rick, and thanks f'r all the drinks."

The rain had just about stopped when Weldon pulled out of the parking lot and turned down the two-lane blacktop road. He felt wonderful. He was in the homestretch! Stan and Eddie were great guys. He would drive down sometime and look them up. They would have another party. He would bring Livvie. Stan and Eddie would like her. Everyone liked Livvie.

He didn't expect Livvie to be at Loon Lake when he got there; she was probably away at school somewhere. But she would be home one of these weekends, Thanksgiving, at the latest. Which was fine. It would give him time to take care of his business. He would throw a big party for her. But what if she didn't drink. No problem; he would teach her. Start her off on something tasty, a Tom Collins, maybe, or a whiskey sour. They both had lemon juice and sugar in them, and the whiskey sour was garnished with a slice of orange and a maraschino cherry.

A whiskey sour had been his first drink, at a neighborhood wedding reception, in a tent, where they had an open bar. Ever since junior high, he had watched other guys get drunk on beer or wine coolers and then puke their guts out. And he could never understand what they saw in it. And then at the wedding reception, Mr. Peters, their next-door neighbor, had handed him a drink and said, "Try this, Weldon. It's very tasty."

And so he had tried one. And then another. And still another. It was a revelation. He had discovered a wonderful new dimension in life, a dimension that would--

Red flasher light!

He glanced at the speedometer. Sixty. It was a forty-five zone; he had seen a sign. Oh, God! He'd screwed up. Badly. He hadn't been paying attention to details. He hadn't been anticipating. But the bastards weren't going to get him. Not now. Not with Loon Lake so close he could practically smell it. An amber traffic light was just ahead. Was it blinking him a message? That was the shortest way to the freeway, Eddie had said. The red flasher light was coming up fast behind him, and he could hear a siren. *Eee-ow, eee-ow, eee-ow.* He waited till the last possible moment, then threw the T-bird into a violent left turn, tires screeching, and gunned it.

It was a hilly road--Eddie hadn't mentioned that--short, steep hills, like a mini-rollercoaster. Up and down. Up and down. Whee! *One hill, two hills, three hills, four.*/*Up and down and lookit me soar*! Whee! Coming over the next hill--Oh, my God! There's something in the road! Was it that goddamn farmer again?

"YOU GODDAMN FARMER!" he shouted.

He was braking now. There was a series of noises, funny noises, like a stick being run over a picket fence, only soft sounds, dull sounds. Everything was moving in slow motion. The car was skidding, but, hell, that was no problem. He would whip it around and be over the next hill before that flasher light was in sight. He knew how to drive this mother, this sweet, lovely T-bird.

A TREE!

Where did that damn tree come from? That big, black, ugly, wet tree? *Goin' home to my dar--*

YEAGER: And that's all I remember.

BECKER: The car rolled before it hit the tree. The roof was crushed, but your seat belt held. Otherwise, your brains would've been scrambled.

YEAGER: What happens now?

BECKER: Nothing, until we're able to get you over to Judge Breakey. He'll bind you over to circuit court for trial.

YEAGER: When will that be?

BECKER: Whenever Doctor Weng says you can be moved. I'd hate to see your hospital bill. You're costing the taxpayers a bundle.

YEAGER: I'm sorry.

BECKER: Sure you are. Sorry, sorry, sorry. Well, that's it for now. Let the record show that the prisoner gave this statement freely and without duress. Correct, Yeager?

YEAGER: Yes, sir.

BECKER: End of interrogation.

He turned off the tape recorder and pressed the button on the call box.

"This is Lieutenant Becker. I'm finished. Please tell Officer Bibich."

He unplugged the tape recorder and removed the mike from Weldon's gown.

"Miss Wetherby, you're free to resume your normal routine."

"Thank you, lieutenant." She wrapped a blood pressure cuff around Weldon's right arm. "How are you feeling, Weldon?"

"Okay, I guess."

"Open your mouth, please," she said. "I want to take your temperature."

Lieutenant Becker put the tape recorder and his other things back into the carrying case.

"Someone will bring over a copy of your statement for you to sign on Monday," he said. "That was quite a story, Yeager. Pity you didn't turn down that last drink. Those three kids might still be alive."

Officer Bibich came into the room, followed by Dr. Weng,

who was eating a candy bar, a Snickers.

"Wow!" Dr. Weng said. "This room looks like a precinct station after a hard day. Aren't you going to frisk us, lieutenant?"

Lieutenant Becker smiled. "No, just thank you for your cooperation. We'll be getting out of your way now. Nick, how's the game going?"

"Bridgton's losing," Officer Bibich said. "Fourteen-thirteen. They're in the third quarter."

"Just one point, huh?"

"They went for two on the extra point and missed."

"Let's hustle on over there," the lieutenant said. "Doctor Weng, Miss Wetherby--thank you again."

Dr. Weng saw them to the door.

"Uh, by the way, lieutenant," he said, "if you ever need a fast appendectomy, let me know. I moonlight in my garage." Lieutenant Becker laughed. "You'll be the first to know." he said, shaking Dr. Weng's hand. "Good-bye."

Dr. Weng closed the door behind them and leaned back against it.

"Whew!" he said, wiping his brow. "Thank God that's over with. Maybe now we can start being a hospital again. Martha, may I see Junior's chart?"

He went to the bed and gave Weldon a quick onceover.

"Well, how're you holding up, boy?"

"Pretty good." Weldon said.

"I assume that Lieutenant Becker told you everything?"

"Everything."

"And you probably feel like swallowing cyanide?"

"Something like that."

"Well, that goes with the territory," Dr. Weng said, taking a bite of his candy bar. "But there's another way of looking at it."

"Another philo*th*opher?"

"As a matter of fact, yes. Confucius, the wisest one of all, in my judgment. He said something to the effect that a man who is given a second life owes the world a lot."

"I don't get it," Weldon said.

"It's not a joke, Junior." He pulled a chair up to the bed and sat down. "The others are dead, but you're alive," he said, still chewing. "Doesn't that mean something to you?"

"Like what?"

"Like redemption," Dr. Weng said. "Sure, you could throw yourself out a window or something. That's the easy way. Or you could recognize that you now have a special responsibility, a responsibility to make their deaths mean something."

The conversation was making Weldon edgy. "And how would I do that?" he said.

"Oh, there're lots of ways." Dr. Weng finished his Snickers. "Become a doctor and find a cure for cancer. Become a chemist and discover a new element. Or just become a solid citizen and a force for good in your community. Why, you could even--"

"Doctor Weng," --it was the call box-- *"you're wanted in Emergency."*

"Damn!" He started for the door. "Tell her I'm on my way, Martha. Junior, let the evil of the day be sufficient thereunto. See you Monday."

Miss Wetherby watched him go, amused.

"That man," she said, shaking her head. "He comes and goes like a whirlwind." She lifted the blanket from the foot cradle and checked Weldon's bandages. "Well, it's been quite a day for you, Weldon. How is your pain?"

"Not too bad right now."

"Do you think you could eat something?"

"I don't know. Maybe."

"We'll start you off with clear liquids and see how you handle them. All right?"

"Ye*th*, ma'am."

"Meantime, why don't you watch some television? It might take your mind off things."

"There's probably nothing on but football. I'm getting plenty of that through the window."

"The Grand Rapids station has reruns Saturday afternoons." She turned on the TV and swung the little set around to the bed. "Here's the earphone, Weldon. Now it's time for me to leave. I should've been off duty an hour ago."

"Will you be here tomorrow?"

"I'm off on Sundays, but I'll be here Monday."

Weldon hated to see her go; the other nurses might not be as nice.

"Miss Wetherby?" he said as she was going out.

"Yes, Weldon?"

"You've been very good to me today---" He paused, groping for words, but found none. "Thank you."

Martha Wetherby looked at him for a moment and smiled. "A man I was once going to marry had eyes like yours." There were tears in her eyes again. "He was killed in Vietnam. Good night, Weldon."

As she opened the door, he could see that a different officer was now on duty in the hall, a man this time. The changing of the guard, he thought. And probably another one at midnight, and then another and another . . .

He sighed deeply and slipped the earphone into an ear. An episode of *M*A*S*H* was on. Hawkeye and B.J. were drinking "martinis" from their still. He watched the program, unseeing, remembering the TV programs he and Livvie had watched at Loon Lake, *Mork & Mindy* and *Little House on the Prairie* and *The Waltons*, which was his favorite program of all, because the character Mary Ellen looked like Livvie. "Oh, Weldon, I do not look like her," Livvie had protested. "Mary Ellen has bosoms." Weldon had laughed. "Well, you're going to have them one

93

day, too," he had replied. And in his hayloft dream, she did, round and firm and pointed when he tickled them---

After a beer commercial and one for a used-car dealer, the news came on. The lead story was about a terrorist attack in Beirut. The news bored him. The troubles of Lebanon seemed petty compared to his own. He could see only one ray of hope, the possibility of seeing Livvie. He wasn't worried about that; that was the stuff of poetry, the stricken lovers clasping hands from their hospital beds. "Livvie," he would whisper. "Weldon?" she would answer, her voice weak. "Is it really you?" *"In regional news, this just in from Bridgton. The last surviving victim of that tragic accident Thursday in which four Hillgrove College students were run down by a drunken driver has died."* Maybe this whole thing would work out yet. Livvie would stand by him at his trial and wait for him while he was in prison. *"A Bridgton Memorial Hospital spokesperson said eighteen-year-old Olivia Anne Buhl of Loon Lake died without regaining consciousness."* He would start writing and make a lot of money. When he was paroled, he and Livvie would build a place on Up Holly Bay. They would give it a name, Loon Lodge, maybe. *"The car was driven by Weldon E. Yeager, Junior, eighteen, of Springhurst, Illinois."* There would be a paneled den for his writing, and on cold winter nights, they would sit around the fireplace, sipping mulled cider with rum in it. *"Yeager, a police prisoner at Bridgton Memorial, has been charged with four counts of second-degree murder."*

He turned off the TV. A roar went up from the stadium, and the band struck up a fight song. His eyes were brimming with tears.

He needed a drink. God, how he needed a drink.

Could the tragedy of
Weldon Yeager have
been prevented? Does he
have any hope for a use-
ful and fulfilling life?
The answer to both ques-
tions is an emphatic:

YES!

THE ROAD TO RECOVERY

introducing

ALCOHOLICS FOR ALCOHOLICS

AFA

and

THE EIGHT STEPS TO SOBRIETY AND A BETTER YOU

A NEW DIMENSION

To the Reader:

In issuing the second edition of *Binge* (revised), the editors and editorial consultants of Daisy Hill Press feel a strong sense of mission.

AFA/Eight Steps, we are convinced, is the most promising self-help, group-therapy, alcoholic recovery program in the entire world.

We base our confidence on the simple fact that all other such programs, both secular and religious, were developed by persons who, at the time, were still under the lingering effects of alcohol; hence they had no real perspective on their own problems, let alone the problem of widespread alcoholism.

For instance, the founders of Alcoholics Anonymous were less than a year from roaring drunkenness—barroom brawls, DTs (delirium tremens) hospital stays—when they devised the religious Twelve Steps. Likewise, the founders of Women/Men for Sobriety, Rational Recovery, and other secular recovery groups were in the early stages of recovery, which may explain their ineffectiveness.

By contrast, Charles Ferry has learned the hard way that long periods of alcohol abuse (25 years for him) have an insidious mental effect on a person, a fact not fully understood by substance-abuse professionals.

Alcohol is a mind-altering drug. Prolonged use of it can twist a person's thinking in every conceivable way, distorting relationships with family, friends, associates, in major matters, trifling matter. It is such a gradual, diabolical process that abusers are unaware how warped their thinking had become until they begin to recover.

Moreover, Ferry has found that an alcoholic doesn't start

thinking clearly again until after 10 years or more of sobriety. But the central weakness in ALL recovery programs, secular and religious, he has learned, is that they have a single goal: sobriety. They are unconcerned with the whole person, with personal growth. Ferry saw an urgent need for a new approach to alcoholic recovery and resolved to do something about it.

And so, after 25 years of alcoholic horrors, followed by 28 years of successful recovery, which have included voluminous research, Charles Ferry possessed the perspective, the insights, and the unique professional skills needed to develop an entirely new dimension in substance-abuse treatment—a program that promotes independence and empowers alcoholics to take charge of their own lives, that can be modified or revised to cope with any personal problem, that has already been adapted for an encouraging suicide-prevention program (page 27).

Alcoholics For Alcoholics is a concept, not an organization. It is the first and only alcoholic recovery program entirely oriented to the individual. There is no organizational structure beyond *The Eight Steps to Sobriety and a Better You.* In order to reach as many concerned persons as possible, Charles Ferry has waived all rights to *The Eight Steps* and placed them in the public domain.

The Eight Steps build confidence and self-understanding. As you will learn, anyone may start an *AFA/Eight Steps* group—a foreman, a clerk, an executive; a student, a teacher, a parent. Meetings may be held anytime, anywhere: at home, at work, at school, indoors, outdoors.

There is great flexibility. New steps may be added to cover any abused substance, with the program becoming *Addicts For Addicts/Eight Steps to a Clean and Better You.*

Alcoholics For Alcoholics means exactly that. Persons who share the same background are drawn together to dis-

B 3

cuss a common problem: alcohol. That is the key to effective group-therapy. While all other recovery programs have a single goal—sobriety—with *AFA*, sobriety is just the beginning. The ultimate goal, through personal growth, is not merely a sober person but a *better* person.

All of which explains why we strongly feel that *AFA/Eight Steps* introduces an exciting concept that points the way to a major turning point in the fight against alcoholism—and other problems—worldwide.

We hope it will be a turning point in your life, too.

The Editors

HOW IT ALL STARTED

AFA/EIGHT STEPS is the product of pain and anguish.

It grew out of the troubled life of award-winning author Charles Ferry, which is detailed in his autobiography (Gale Research, Inc.: *Something about the Author Autobiography Series*, vol. 20), which is available at most public libraries throughout the English-speaking world.

It tells about Ferry's disturbed childhood, his enuresis (he wet the bed until he was 14 years old), about his World War II service as a 17-year-old aerial gunner in the U.S. Navy, where his drinking began.

After the war, a brilliant career in journalism was shattered by a growing addiction to alcohol. Ferry went on to drink his way into 14 different jails, three of them twice and one of them the largest walled jail in the world: the State Prison of Southern Michigan. For three years, he lived with screams in the night and the rumble of heavy steel doors. One week, in solitary confinement, he lived in a darkened cell where he lost track of time.

Why was he sent to prison? Forgery, to get money for alcohol. But that was only the tip of the iceberg. Prison was the disgraceful culmination of a six-month, nine-state drunken binge, during which he was a mini crime wave— two stolen cars, one abandoned, one totaled; five break-ins, most of them senseless; bad checks; larceny whenever there was an opportunity to steal something—anything to keep alcohol flowing through his bloodstream.

After prison, he resumed his dissolute habits, but with one important difference—he now had a loving wife, who urged him to try Alcoholics Anonymous, which he did.

But he found the bleak meetings in church basements depressing and AA's strong emphasis on dependence discouraging. He continued drinking.

Finally, in 1970, at age 43, through his own resources, he triumphed over the problem. He is now in his 29th year of successful recovery.

How did he do it? Quite simply, he did it *his* way. And he has compressed his recovery into eight simple steps that he knows will spare countless people the agony of alcoholism: *The Eight Steps to Sobriety and a Better You.*

To learn all about them, simply turn the page.

First Step. We admitted that alcohol abuse was destroying our lives.

Second Step. We made an honest examination of our failings in life and of the harmful things we have done, to ourselves and to others, while under the influence of alcohol.

Third Step. We learned to speak openly of the circumstances of our lives, without resentment or recrimination.

Fourth Step. We learned that the power to change our lives, which is love, love of self and love of others, is within us.

Fifth Step. We made a searching inventory of our lives to identify all of the good that is within us.

Sixth Step. We resolved to be true to the best that is in us and to help other people, recognizing that in helping others, our own problems fall away.

Seventh Step. We learned that in writing honestly about our lives and our problems, we would come to understand them.

Eighth Step. We learned not to drink one day at a time and to let tomorrow take care of itself.

THE EIGHT STEPS TO SOBRIETY AND A BETTER YOU

THE EIGHT STEPS TO SOBRIETY AND A BETTER YOU

THE EIGHT STEPS TO SOBRIETY AND A BETTER YOU

THE EIGHT STEPS TO SOBRIETY AND A BETTER YOU

THE EIGHT STEPS TO SOBRIETY AND A BETTER YOU

THE EIGHT STEPS TO SOBRIETY AND A BETTER YOU

THE EIGHT STEPS TO SOBRIETY AND A BETTER YOU

THE EIGHT STEPS TO SOBRIETY AND A BETTER YOU

THE EIGHT STEPS TO SOBRIETY AND A BETTER YOU

WORKING *THE EIGHT STEPS*

First Step. We admitted that alcohol abuse was destroying our lives.

Physicians and psychiatrists bicker endlessly over classifications and criteria to define persons who abuse alcohol. Problem drinkers? Alcohol dependent? Alcoholics?
AFA asks a very simple question. Alcohol is a mind-altering drug. Is its use causing a continuing problem in your life? If so, you are abusing it. Any person who abuses alcohol, to the extent of the abuse, is an alcoholic.

THE EIGHT STEPS TO SOBRIETY AND A BETTER YOU

THE EIGHT STEPS TO SOBRIETY AND A BETTER YOU

THE EIGHT STEPS TO SOBRIETY AND A BETTER YOU

THE EIGHT STEPS TO SOBRIETY AND A BETTER YOU

THE EIGHT STEPS TO SOBRIETY AND A BETTER YOU

THE EIGHT STEPS TO SOBRIETY AND A BETTER YOU

THE EIGHT STEPS TO SOBRIETY AND A BETTER YOU

THE EIGHT STEPS TO SOBRIETY AND A BETTER YOU

THE EIGHT STEPS TO SOBRIETY AND A BETTER YOU

Second Step. We made an honest examination of our failings in life and of the harmful things we have done, to ourselves and to others, while under the influence of alcohol.

The Second Step is truth. It involves painful honesty and courage, the courage to speak openly about the horrors alcohol abuse has caused in our lives—the lies, the deceptions, the cruelties, the reverberating impact on friends and family, on virtually everyone we know and respect. In a word, the Second Step is confession, which is essential to emotional healing. Working it may cause tears, but it will leave you with a great sense of relief.

THE EIGHT STEPS TO SOBRIETY AND A BETTER YOU

THE EIGHT STEPS TO SOBRIETY AND A BETTER YOU

THE EIGHT STEPS TO SOBRIETY AND A BETTER YOU

THE EIGHT STEPS TO SOBRIETY AND A BETTER YOU

THE EIGHT STEPS TO SOBRIETY AND A BETTER YOU

THE EIGHT STEPS TO SOBRIETY AND A BETTER YOU

THE EIGHT STEPS TO SOBRIETY AND A BETTER YOU

THE EIGHT STEPS TO SOBRIETY AND A BETTER YOU

THE EIGHT STEPS TO SOBRIETY AND A BETTER YOU

Third Step. We learned to speak openly of the circumstances of our lives, without resentment or recrimination.

Alcoholics unconsciously use resentments and recriminations to avoid the truth about themselves. Criticism of their behavior offends them, triggering strong resentments against their critics. This can be a brooding thing.

Alcoholics also have a strong need to assess blame. When something goes wrong, it's always somebody else's fault, never their own. If an alcoholic is fired from his/her job, it's because someone was out to get them, never because of their drinking or poor job performance.

As with Second Step, the Third Step is bedrock honesty. No excuses, no rationalizations, just the simple, unvarnished truth about your life.

THE EIGHT STEPS TO SOBRIETY AND A BETTER YOU

THE EIGHT STEPS TO SOBRIETY AND A BETTER YOU

THE EIGHT STEPS TO SOBRIETY AND A BETTER YOU

THE EIGHT STEPS TO SOBRIETY AND A BETTER YOU

THE EIGHT STEPS TO SOBRIETY AND A BETTER YOU

THE EIGHT STEPS TO SOBRIETY AND A BETTER YOU

THE EIGHT STEPS TO SOBRIETY AND A BETTER YOU

THE EIGHT STEPS TO SOBRIETY AND A BETTER YOU

THE EIGHT STEPS TO SOBRIETY AND A BETTER YOU

Fourth Step.   We learned that the power to change our lives, which is love, love of self and love of others, is within us.

The Fourth Step introduces the alcoholic to the power of love. Along with the Sixth Step, it is the heart of the *AFA/Eight Steps* program. But while it is a loving Step, it is the toughest Step of all, for reasons we shall explain.

It is a psychological truism that all persons, regardless of their mental or physical endowment, possess a great, latent inner strength that they can draw on in times of grave crisis or challenge. Physicians see this quite commonly in their patients—mind over matter. It is also surprisingly common in substance abusers.

In developing the *AFA/Eight Steps* program, Charles Ferry identified that latent strength as love—love of self, love of others. He concluded that any recovery program that fails to tap an alcoholic's inner resources is doomed to fail.

Ferry cites a niece, an attractive, accomplished young woman, as an example. She got involved with a Las Vegas gambler, who introduced her to cocaine. She developed a $1000-per-day habit (they were selling the stuff).
It took a while, but she finally broke with the gambler and proceeded to kick the habit *with no outside help whatsoever*. How did she do it? Love, self-love, which is the tough part of the Fourth Step.

You see, alcoholics, by definition, are not self-lovers; they are self-abusers. They fill their bodies with a mind-altering poison that produces vomit, flatulence, diarrhea, red eyes, trembling hands, delirium tremens, grave medical problems, and finally—death.

How does an alcoholic develop self-love? That's what *AFA/Eight Steps* is all about—activating the latent strength within you, which is love, love of self, love of others.

You're probably feeling better about yourself already. And when you start working the Fifth Step, you'll learn that you are really a very special person, a person who is well worth loving.

B 15

THE EIGHT STEPS TO SOBRIETY AND A BETTER YOU

THE EIGHT STEPS TO SOBRIETY AND A BETTER YOU

THE EIGHT STEPS TO SOBRIETY AND A BETTER YOU

THE EIGHT STEPS TO SOBRIETY AND A BETTER YOU

THE EIGHT STEPS TO SOBRIETY AND A BETTER YOU

THE EIGHT STEPS TO SOBRIETY AND A BETTER YOU

THE EIGHT STEPS TO SOBRIETY AND A BETTER YOU

THE EIGHT STEPS TO SOBRIETY AND A BETTER YOU

THE EIGHT STEPS TO SOBRIETY AND A BETTER YOU

Fifth Step. We made a searching inventory of our lives to identify all of the good that is within us.

The Fifth Step can be profound psychotherapy. If you work it honestly and work it well, you will relive your life and come to understand yourself.

We usually have no difficulty in recalling the negatives in our lives. But the positive factors that build character and form personality are usually forgotten.

In a word, the Fifth Step is remembrance. In working it, blot out all of the negatives; concentrate only on the positive. Nothing is too small; nothing is irrelevant. There is a single criterion: *good.*

We suggest that you begin with your earliest recollections and then section your life into periods—childhood, grade school, adolescence, high school, college, employment, marriage, and so on.

Relive your relationships with family and friends, your acts of kindness to others, your many achievements in life. Taking out the trash weekly at age 11 is just as important as winning a major job promotion at age 30.

Make the Fifth Step an ongoing part of your life, then share your insights at *AFA* meetings. Everyone will benefit from such a discussion—particularly *you.*

THE EIGHT STEPS TO SOBRIETY AND A BETTER YOU

THE EIGHT STEPS TO SOBRIETY AND A BETTER YOU

THE EIGHT STEPS TO SOBRIETY AND A BETTER YOU

THE EIGHT STEPS TO SOBRIETY AND A BETTER YOU

THE EIGHT STEPS TO SOBRIETY AND A BETTER YOU

THE EIGHT STEPS TO SOBRIETY AND A BETTER YOU

THE EIGHT STEPS TO SOBRIETY AND A BETTER YOU

THE EIGHT STEPS TO SOBRIETY AND A BETTER YOU

THE EIGHT STEPS TO SOBRIETY AND A BETTER YOU

Sixth Step. We resolved to be true to the best that is in us and to help other people, recognizing that in helping others, our own problems fall away.

In developing the Sixth Step, Charles Ferry drew heavily on the wisdom of William Shakespeare, from whom he learned a rule of life that he recommends to everyone, not just alcoholics. *Hamlet*, Act I, Scene 3. Polonius, the father of Ophelia, is speaking:

This above all, to thine own self be true,
And it must follow, as the night the day,
Thou canst not then be false to any man.

Ferry simply revised those words and added an important proviso:

This above all, be true to the best that is in you
And help other people.

The Sixth Step is a living expression of the Fifth Step (all of the good that is within you), as well as of the Fourth Step (love of self, love of others).

Everyone needs help. The opportunities for giving of yourself are virtually limitless—community programs, youth programs, shelters, ad infinitum. Or you can reach out with love and caring to someone in your personal sphere, someone who is hurting.

Love begets love. It reverberates—and heals.

THE EIGHT STEPS TO SOBRIETY AND A BETTER YOU

THE EIGHT STEPS TO SOBRIETY AND A BETTER YOU

THE EIGHT STEPS TO SOBRIETY AND A BETTER YOU

THE EIGHT STEPS TO SOBRIETY AND A BETTER YOU

THE EIGHT STEPS TO SOBRIETY AND A BETTER YOU

THE EIGHT STEPS TO SOBRIETY AND A BETTER YOU

THE EIGHT STEPS TO SOBRIETY AND A BETTER YOU

THE EIGHT STEPS TO SOBRIETY AND A BETTER YOU

THE EIGHT STEPS TO SOBRIETY AND A BETTER YOU

Seventh Step. We learned that in writing honestly about our lives and our problems, we would come to understand them.

The great American poet Emily Dickenson (1830-86) once wrote:

"How can I know what I think until I read what I have written?"

Without knowing it, she was articulating a basic truth of modern psychiatry: Writing is the best psychotherapy there is.

But again, as with all of *The Eight Steps*, the bedrock is honesty. That's what Emily Dickenson meant: Writing involves deep introspection about one's thoughts and feelings. The result is—*truth*. And in working the Seventh Step, that's what you will achieve—the truth about yourself.

But I can't write, you're thinking to yourself. Oh, but you can. If you can write a letter, you can write for personal therapy.

And that's a good way to begin, with letters—letters to yourself. Write about your problems; write about your *true* feelings. If you have hateful feelings toward your husband or wife, your boss, a son or daughter—let it all spill out. Be brutally frank.

Date everything you write. Save everything you write. It will be a measure of your personal growth. For in future weeks or months, you will reread what you have written and learn that your feelings are changing, that the hate is draining out of you, that you are becoming a better person—which is what *The Eight Steps* are all about.

THE EIGHT STEPS TO SOBRIETY AND A BETTER YOU

THE EIGHT STEPS TO SOBRIETY AND A BETTER YOU

THE EIGHT STEPS TO SOBRIETY AND A BETTER YOU

THE EIGHT STEPS TO SOBRIETY AND A BETTER YOU

THE EIGHT STEPS TO SOBRIETY AND A BETTER YOU

THE EIGHT STEPS TO SOBRIETY AND A BETTER YOU

THE EIGHT STEPS TO SOBRIETY AND A BETTER YOU

THE EIGHT STEPS TO SOBRIETY AND A BETTER YOU

THE EIGHT STEPS TO SOBRIETY AND A BETTER YOU

Eighth Step. We learned not to drink one day at a time and to let tomorrow take care of itself.

One of the nicest things about the *AFA/Eight Steps* program is that you don't have to quit drinking for an extended period, just for one day.

Whenever you feel an urge to go out and belt down a few, just say to yourself, "No, I'll put it off until tomorrow."

And if you do slip, it's no big deal; tomorrow is another day. However, your high from the alcohol will be dulled by the knowledge that you're playing with fire.

Also, when drinking after a long period of abstinence, your hangover will be more severe. Body chemistry.

Oh yes, you will feel rotten about yourself.

STARTING AN *EIGHT STEPS* GROUP

WHO CAN START A GROUP?

Students, teachers, mothers, fathers, husbands, wives, sons, daughters, employers, employees, friends, acquaintances—virtually anyone.

HOW DO I GO ABOUT STARTING A GROUP?

If you have a drinking problem, you know others who have been having trouble with alcohol. Simply give them a copy of *The Eight Steps* and say, "Hey, let's give it a try, okay?"

Or it could be a situation within your own family—an alcoholic mother, father, sister, brother. Do the same thing. Pass around *Eight Steps* cards and say, "Why don't we all sit down and talk about this?"

Of course, the best way would be to give the problem person a copy of this book to read. Whichever way you choose, be prepared for instant denial. Avoid pressuring the person and putting him/her on the defense. All alcoholics *know* they are addicted to alcohol. Let them come to terms with themselves. You'll be surprised how quickly even the most troubled drinker will start responding to *The Eight Steps*. Just a casual reading of the Steps will start a person—*any* person, alcoholic or no—thinking seriously and honestly about their lives.

WHERE CAN A GROUP MEET?

Virtually anywhere. At schools, after classes. At work, after quitting time (most employers will gladly make a meeting room available). Meetings can be held in private rooms at restaurants; even better, at coffee houses.

You will have marvelous flexibility in scheduling

meetings, but the best place of all is in the relaxed atmosphere of a private home, where meetings can be followed by fellowship and refreshments.

WHAT ABOUT EIGHT STEPS CARDS?

Every member should have one. You may simply photocopy the Steps in this book. Many copiers now enlarge or reduce while they copy, which makes it easy to make copies large enough to use at meetings or small enough to fit in one's pocket, purse, wallet—whichever.

But the best way is to *memorize* the Steps and make them a part of your daily life.

HOW DOES A TYPICAL MEETING WORK?

Again, there is great flexibility. Meetings can be conducted any way you wish. Usually, meetings are private (but they can be open and involve friends or family members). The group appoints a leader to chair the meeting. With a new group, the Steps are usually worked in sequence, one step per meeting (or you may spend several meetings on a single step). After that, the group may vote on which Step to discuss.

The leader calls on each member for her/his comments. At first, participants will feel shy and self-conscious and be reluctant to speak. But in any group of two or more persons, one will be a leader. And that's all it takes, one person to break the ice, so to speak. Then the others will join in eagerly, even volubly.

The important thing is for each person to speak openly and honestly about their problems. After the individual comments, there may be a group discussion. The leader then announce the date and time of the next meeting (after consulting with other members) and adjourns the session.

Meetings in private homes can be truly marvelous experiences. They can bring families closer together. For teenagers, they are usually followed by a social hour, with music and dancing, soft drinks and pizza. This generates enthusiasm for *AFA/Eight Steps* that filters out into the community, building respect for the way young people are trying to turn their lives around.

Alcoholism can be cured or arrested only by the alcoholic. There are no magic wands. But *The Eight Steps* chart the course to a wonderful new life for troubled drinkers.

CAN *THE EIGHT STEPS* BE WORKED PRIVATELY?

They certainly can. In fact, that is the basic strength of the *AFA/Eight Steps* program.

The steps are not just for meetings; they are for *you*, they become a part of your daily life.

You can work them anytime, anywhere, at home, on vacation, in far-away places—while driving your car; while on boring flight to some distant city; while taking a shower or sitting on the throne of thought; or best of all, in the twilight zone as you're drifting off to sleep at night.

There are no free lunches in life. You will get out of *The Eight Steps* only what you put into them, no more, no less.

But if your goal is truly sobriety and a better you—you can begin this instant.

Good Luck!

ADAPTABILITY OF *THE EIGHT STEPS*

THE EIGHT STEPS concept is not limited to substance abuse; it can be adapted to cope with virtually any problem. For instance, in his novel *Life!* (fighting death by celebrating life), Charles Ferry deals with the trauma of suicidal persons simply by revising Steps One, Two, Three, and Eight, thus providing a pathway to hope, as follows:

EIGHT STEPS TO A BRIGHTER TOMORROW

Step 1. We admitted we were angry and depressed and wanted to end our lives.

Step 2. We made an honest examination of the circumstances of our lives, without resentment or recrimination.

Step 3. We learned to speak openly of our hurts and sorrows, to our families and to our friends, and to ask for their help.

Step 4. We learned that the power to change our lives, which is love, love of self and love of others, is within us.

Step 5. We made a searching inventory of our lives to identify all of the good that is within us.

Step 6. We resolved to be true to the best that is in us and to help other people, recognizing that in helping others, our own problems fall away.

Step 7. We learned that in writing honestly about our lives and our problems, we would come to understand them.

Step 8. We learned to sleep on our decisions, aware that tomorrow may be—and usually is—a brighter day.

THE EIGHT STEPS TO SOBRIETY AND A BETTER YOU

THE EIGHT STEPS TO SOBRIETY AND A BETTER YOU

THE EIGHT STEPS TO SOBRIETY AND A BETTER YOU

THE EIGHT STEPS TO SOBRIETY AND A BETTER YOU

THE EIGHT STEPS TO SOBRIETY AND A BETTER YOU

THE EIGHT STEPS TO SOBRIETY AND A BETTER YOU

THE EIGHT STEPS TO SOBRIETY AND A BETTER YOU

THE EIGHT STEPS TO SOBRIETY AND A BETTER YOU

THE EIGHT STEPS TO SOBRIETY AND A BETTER YOU

"A LIGHT AT THE END OF THE TUNNEL."

We'll close this book with a final message to our readers.

By now, you probably understand why everyone at Daisy Hill Press feels a strong sense of mission. *AFA/Eight Steps*, we are convinced, is a major breakthrough in the ongoing fight against alcoholism—the first and only program of its type, not only in America, but in the entire world.

The first? You can't be serious, you're thinking.

Oh, but we are. You see, ever since 1936, when alcoholism as an illness came out of the closet, there has been a general public assumption that recovery groups, hospitals, and other treatment centers have been engaged in programmed group therapy.

This is a false assumption. The plain truth is that, with the cost of alcoholism to our society soaring out of sight ($100 billion per year and steadily rising), there has *never* been, in America or anyplace else, a self-/group-therapy program for recovering alcoholics—*spontaneous* therapy, yes; but no *program* with specific steps to reach specific goals.

For instance, major (and expensive) substance-abuse treatment centers—Betty Ford in California, Hazelden in Minnesota, Maplegrove in Michigan, and scores of others—are primarily detoxification centers, offering physical rehabilitation, counseling, and fellowship, but no programmed group-therapy. Likewise, the various self-help recovery groups, both religious and secular, offer no therapy prgram, only fellowship and prayers or principles.

Against that historical backdrop comes a simple, inexpensive program that points the way not merely to recovery but to a better life, a program that offers hope.

As one of our strongest supporters, Betsy Fried*, a tireless warrior against alcoholism and substance abuse in general, puts it:

"*AFA/Eight Steps* is a light at the end of the tunnel for America's alcohol crisis."

You can help keep that light burning brightly. How? Spread the word.

THE EDITORS

*Young adult specialist at the Toledo/Lucas County (Ohio) Public Library.